Access to History

General Editor: Keith Randell

Louis XIV, France and Europe 1661-1715

Richard Wilkinson

Hodder & Stoughton

LONDON SYDNEY AUCKLAND

The cover illustration shows a portrait of Louis XIV by Rigaud. (Courtesy of Services de la Réunion Photographie des Musées Nationaux, Paris.)

Some other titles in the series:

Charles V: Ruler, Dynast and Defender of the State, 1500-58
Stewart Macdonald
ISBN 0 340 53558 X

Spain: Rise and Decline, 1474-1643
Jill Kilsby
ISBN 0 340 51807 3

Europe and the Enlightened Despots
Walter Oppenheim
ISBN 0 340 53559 8

Habsburgs and Hohenzollerns, 1713-1786
Walter Oppenheim
ISBN 0 340 55045 7

France in Revolution
Duncan Townson
ISBN 0 340 53494 X

Napoleon, France and Europe
Andrina Stiles
ISBN 0 340 57375 9

For C.A.W.

British Library Cataloguing in Publication Data

Wilkinson, Richard
   France and Louis XIV, 1661-1715. –
   (Access to History Series)
   I. Title II. Series
   944
ISBN 0-340-57511-5

First published 1993

Impression number	10	9	8	7	6	5	4	3	2	1
Year		1998	1997	1996	1995	1994	1993			

Typeset by Sempringham publishing, Bedford
Printed in Great Britain for the educational publishing division of Hodder & Stoughton Ltd, Mill Road, Dunton Green, Sevenoaks, Kent by Page Bros (Norwich) Ltd

Contents

Preface

To the general reader

Although the Access to History series has been designed with the needs of students studying the subject at higher examination levels very much in mind, it also has a great deal to offer the general reader. The main body of the text (i.e. ignoring the Study Guides at the ends of chapters) forms a readable and yet stimulating survey of a coherent topic as studied by historians. However, each author's aim has not merely been to provide a clear explanation of what happened in the past (to interest and inform): it has also been assumed that most readers wish to be stimulated into thinking further about the topic and to form opinions of their own about the significance of the events that are described and discussed (to be challenged). Thus, although no prior knowledge of the topic is expected on the reader's part, she or he is treated as an intelligent and thinking person throughout. The author tends to share ideas and possibilities with the reader, rather than passing on numbers of so-called 'historical truths'.

To the student reader

There are many ways in which the series can be used by students studying History at a higher level. It will, therefore, be worthwhile thinking about your own study strategy before you start your work on this book. Obviously, your strategy will vary depending on the aim you have in mind, and the time for study that is available to you.

If, for example, you want to acquire a general overview of the topic in the shortest possible time, the following approach will probably be the most effective:

1 Read chapter 1 and think about its contents.
2 Read the 'Making notes' section at the end of chapter 2 and decide whether it is necessary for you to read this chapter.
3 If it is, read the chapter, stopping at each heading or * to note down the main points that have been made.
4 Repeat stage 2 (and stage 3 where appropriate) for all the other chapters.

If, however, your aim is to gain a thorough grasp of the topic, taking however much time is necessary to do so, you may benefit from carrying out the same procedure with each chapter, as follows:

1 Read the chapter as fast as you can, and preferably at one sitting.
2 Study the flow diagram at the end of the chapter, ensuring that you understand the general 'shape' of what you have just read.

3 Read the 'Making notes' section (and the 'Answering essay questions' section, if there is one) and decide what further work you need to do on the chapter. In particularly important sections of the book, this will involve reading the chapter a second time and stopping at each heading and * to think about (and to write a summary of) what you have just read.

4 Attempt the 'Source-based questions' section. It will sometimes be sufficient to think through your answers, but additional understanding will often be gained by forcing yourself to write them down.

When you have finished the main chapters of the book, study the 'Further Reading' section and decide what additional reading (if any) you will do on the topic.

This book has been designed to help make your studies both enjoyable and successful. If you can think of ways in which this could have been done more effectively, please write to tell me. In the meantime, I hope that you will gain greatly from your study of History.

Keith Randell

CHAPTER 1

Introduction: The Study of Louis XIV

1 Why has Louis XIV been so much Studied?

Louis XIV (1638-1715) was King of France for 72 years - the longest reign in European history. He was only a child of five at his accession in 1643, he was in personal control of the government from 1661 until his death. Furthermore, not only did Louis reign for a very long time; he was also a masterful ruler who was determined to achieve his goals. Although total success eluded him, the 'Sun King', as he liked to be called, certainly stamped his personality on his age and dominated Europe for half a century.

Inevitably such a formidable ruler has provoked controversy. Indeed, Louis XIV deliberately adopted a high profile, welcoming fame and notoriety; a sophisticated media campaign publicised and positively exaggerated the achievements of France and her glorious monarch. Some contemporaries were impressed, and slavishly imitated the Sun King. Others hated France and her ruler. Disagreement has raged since Louis' death, fuelling an ever-increasing literary battle of words. No wonder the Sun King has been so much studied.

Readers of this book will be encouraged to form their own opinions about the key issues of Louis XIV's reign. Traditionally these have revolved round the twin themes of the development of absolutism in France and the French struggle for European ascendancy.

The development of absolutism (constitutionally unlimited government) was the French monarchy's response to a period of royal weakness and widespread instability in the second half of the sixteenth century. In 1589 the Valois dynasty expired when the namby-pamby Henri III was assassinated. The man with the best claim to the succession was Henri of Navarre, the leading Bourbon prince. There was nothing effeminate about this extrovert, popular soldier. Henri IV, as he became, founded the tradition of strong, monarchical government which reached its apogee under his grandson, Louis XIV. It was essentially this system, often known as the *ancien régime,* which was abolished by the French Revolution starting in 1789. The development of French royal power contrasted with the emasculation of the English Crown - a contrast emphasised by historians who hero-worshipped the English opposition to the Stuarts and despised French subservience to the Bourbons.

The reassertion of royal power by the Bourbon kings coincided with an aggressive foreign policy. Both contemporaries and historians have interpreted this assertion of French power as a bid for European ascendancy. The sixteenth century had belonged to Spain. Now France challenged the European hegemony of the Spanish Habsburgs, allied to their Austrian cousins, the Holy Roman Emperors. Significantly the seventeenth century has often been called *le grand siècle*, recognition of the success of French imperialism. However, this apparent attempt to dominate Europe was checked by France's enemies who came to distrust the ambitions of Louis XIV in particular.

Attempts to understand the reign are complicated by the fact that fashions change. On the whole, eighteenth-century commentators admired Louis XIV as one of the earliest 'enlightened despots' - monarchs who put their subjects' interests first. On the other hand, in the nineteenth and twentieth centuries historians influenced by democratic liberalism have condemned Louis XIV's oppression of the rights of the individual, his attempts to repress freedom of thought, expression and worship, and his excessive resort to force, both at home and abroad. 'Enlightened despotism' became 'absolutism', a term of abuse implying that the ruler was a selfish, arbitrary tyrant, a forerunner of modern totalitarianism. More recently, however, historians have stressed the limitations on Louis' power. They have pointed out that 'absolutism' was not a seventeenth-century word, questioning indeed whether it can usefully be applied at all to Louis XIV's France. The reader will have to decide if this revisionism is justified or has gone too far.

Similarly with Louis XIV's foreign policy. For liberal, freedom-loving opponents of naked aggression it was all so simple. Looking back into history there was a clearly visible, sinister procession: Philip II of Spain, Louis XIV, Napoleon, the Kaiser, Hitler. All were tyrants and really there was little to choose between them. All aimed at the domination of Europe, if not the world, and all failed, thanks to the intervention of Almighty God and/or the Anglo-Saxons, according to your point of view. On the other hand revisionists argue that Louis XIV had limited, sensible aims, that he was frustrated by vindictive and jealous opponents and that he was more sinned against than sinning. While French historians have predictably hailed Louis XIV as a national hero and a dedicated patriot, historians outside France have also defended Louis' foreign policy, emphasising his caution and the war-like ambitions of his enemies, especially the Emperor Leopold and William of Orange. Again, you will be invited to come to your own conclusions.

Ever-present in the background of these controversies is the basic issue of one's assessment of the Sun King; perhaps it could be summed up, 'Louis XIV - for or against?' While moral judgements are clearly not the historian's business, a high-profiled historical figure such as Louis demands assessment. Were his objectives the right ones? How successful was he in achieving them? If he failed, was that his fault? It is perhaps significant that even his sternest critics concede that Louis XIV was 'a great king' - whatever that means. A modern English historian has said of the French emperor Napoleon III (1852-70) that it is impossible to dislike him but equally impossible to respect him. On a personal note, I confess that I began writing this book with exactly the opposite opinion of Louis XIV. I felt that one probably has to respect the sheer scale of his achievement, yet I had always found it hard to like such an apparent egoist. Frankly, now I am not so sure. At the end of the book, we shall return to the problems of assessing the overall merits and demerits of the Sun King.

Louis XIV is especially worth studying as an illustration of the 'great man' theory of history. The argument here is that history is dominated by highly influential individuals. Simply because of who he was and what his opportunities and responsibilities were, Louis XIV could not help being as it were a 'great man'. However, there are influential historians - often Marxist in sympathy - who prefer to emphasise the role of impersonal forces such as social and economic developments, as against the influence of individual human beings. As Lenin remarked, 'what is the individual but a million over a million?' My own feeling is that, while both approaches have validity, it would be perverse to deny Louis XIV's impact on his times. Simply because he lived so long and because he exercised such considerable power, he is the perfect example of the 'great man' theory in action. When due allowance is made for the importance of significant economic and social forces, Louis XIV's attitudes and objectives, his personal strengths and weaknesses made a significant difference to the history of France and her neighbours between 1661 and 1715. In other words, Louis XIV *mattered*. Because he *mattered* so much, it is important to understand what sort of a man he was, what his background was, and what 'made him tick'. To these issues we now turn.

2 Louis XIV - the Man and his Background

'Respect is the death of history', according to a French historian. In this book you will be invited to adopt a critical approach to Louis XIV who was indeed a fallible king and, like the rest of us, a fallible human being. His background helps us to evaluate the man.

A psychologist would have a field-day with Louis' childhood. To say that he was the product of an unhappy marriage would be an understatement. His parents were totally incompatible: the moody, introverted, boorish, insecure Louis XIII and the Spanish Habsburg Anne of Austria, physically attractive, neat, precise and civilised. They rarely had sexual intercourse or indeed any sort of intercourse, and when Anne became pregnant after twenty years of marriage, it was understandably seen as a miracle; hence Louis XIV's nickname *'le dieu-donné'* ('the gift of God'). After Louis XIII died when his heir was five, the boy was brought up as a member of a very peculiar household, for Anne of Austria, now Queen-Regent, took up with the chief minister, Cardinal Jules Mazarin, a clever, unscrupulous Italian careerist. Anne may indeed have secretly become Mazarin's wife, not an impossibility as he was only in deacon's orders and was therefore not forbidden to marry. They were certainly very fond of each other, perhaps drawn together by their common experience of French xenophobia (dislike of foreigners). Together they supervised the child-king's education, and significantly Mazarin became his god-father.

If Louis XIV now experienced a certain measure of affection and parental attention, in no way did he enjoy a stable upbringing. For between 1648 and 1653 France was torn apart by the series of revolts known as the *Frondes* (*Fronde* means a sling, the catapult wielded by Parisian urchins). First the Paris *parlement* defied the unpopular chief minister, then the nobles joined the hunt, led by members of the royal family including Gaston, the king's uncle, the personification of selfish irresponsibility. Mazarin fled the country, the queen desperately manoeuvred between warring factions, and the boy-king was hustled from one refuge to another. On one occasion he had to pretend to be asleep in bed in order to reassure Parisians that this time he had not managed to escape. Eventually the *Frondes* collapsed as the leaders demonstrated their own inability to co-operate with each other, Mazarin returned from exile and some semblance of royal authority was restored.

Louis XIV acquired his education in the school of life. He was deeply influenced by the *Frondes,* never abandoning his belief in ordered authority as the antidote to chaos. During his troubled boyhood Louis travelled round France, getting to know something of his realm and its people. Mazarin carefully coached his royal pupil in the craft of kingship. Louis learnt from the Cardinal to believe that monarchy was ordained by God, to identify himself with France, to work hard and to take his job seriously. He also learnt to dissimulate, taking on board Mazarin's cynicism and contempt for human motivation.

Louis' formal education was not neglected, although it was as narrow as most aristocratic upbringings tended to be: some ancient but little modern history, a smattering of geography and mathematics, a grounding in Spanish and Italian. Louis always regretted that he was a poor Latinist; but he learnt to speak and write excellent French, which may well have been more use to him. He was taught to ride, shoot and dance, all of which he did well by instinct. From his mother he derived his unquestioning Catholic piety and hatred of heresy, although like her he had no profound grasp of theological issues.

So what emerged from this background, when the Cardinal's death in 1661 inaugurated Louis' personal rule? There is no doubt that nature and upbringing combined to produce an impressive young man. Louis' physical stature - he was only 5'4" - had to be enhanced by high heels, and he further increased his height by wearing luxuriant wigs. However, Louis' lack of inches was in any case compensated for by innate dignity and poise. Furthermore he possessed great charm and affability. He was intelligent, quick on the uptake and possessed a good memory for faces and facts. He had a piquant sense of humour, referring to his emaciated cousin Henrietta of England as 'the Bones of the Holy Innocents' (the little children murdered by Herod).

Louis XIV had remarkable self-control, believing that it was beneath his dignity either to rage or to exult. When he was displeased, he learnt to dissemble so that people were astonished when the blow fell. Very occasionally Louis lost his composure. The courtier Saint-Simon tells how the great king was mortified because his bastard son had displayed cowardice in battle, and vented his rage on a harmless servant:

> On this occasion Louis XIV succumbed to his emotions. As he was leaving the table he happened to notice one of the waiters pocketing a sweet biscuit. That instant, forgetting his royal dignity, cane in hand he rushed at the footman, beat him, abused him and ended by breaking the cane across his shoulder.

The point is that this example of 'kicking the cat' which Saint-Simon described with malicious relish was wholly untypical. Normally Louis greeted disappointments and frustrations with self-restraint.

Louis XIV was a byword for punctilious courtesy. He always raised his hat to women, even to the lowliest chamber-maid. Often this courtesy was based on genuine regard and sympathy for others. Once a gate-keeper was roundly abused by Louis' companions for his tardiness, but Louis checked them by pointing out that the poor man had already been sufficiently punished by his self-evident mortification at delaying the king. If Louis XIV hurt anyone close to him, it was the queen who never came to terms with her husband's infidelities.

Some historians have argued that Louis XIV's sex-life was unimportant. But this is not so. Louis' relations with women undoubtedly affected his conscience, driving him to actions which he might otherwise not have taken. Nor can it be doubted that his promiscuity with Madame de Montespan, his publicly acknowledged royal mistress for twelve years, damaged his reputation with the French public and with the Church; this constituted double adultery as both Louis and the lady were already married. The expense of his various 'households' certainly added to his financial embarrassments. And the last of his mistresses, Madame de Maintenon, unquestionably exercised influence. Council meetings took place in her presence as she shivered in her armchair, specially designed to exclude the draughts in Louis' study, and her favourites were promoted in Church and State.

To record Louis' irregular private life is not to judge him. However, should one be tempted to judge, it is worth remembering that, like so many royal personages, Louis was obliged to marry a wife who did not appeal to him. Maria Theresa, the daughter of Philip IV of Spain, whom Louis married in 1660 by the terms of the Treaty of the Pyrenees, was stupid, plain and gauche. Louis had already experienced real love. He had fallen for Mazarin's niece, Marie Mancini, who was pretty, vivacious and clever. His affection for her was reciprocated. It says much for Mazarin's single-mindedness that not for a moment did he allow himself to be dazzled by such a potential honour for his family. The two young people were ordered to terminate their relationship forthwith. Louis complied, but there is no reason to doubt that he was heart-broken as he journeyed south to escort home his boring, dumpy Spanish bride.

Louis' reaction was to compensate himself elsewhere. He had been introduced to sex in his mid-teens by a nubile laundry-woman; for the next thirty years there was no stopping him. Like his grandfather, Henri IV, Louis was oversexed and he enjoyed the favours of numerous mistresses, begetting several bastards. Three women were openly acknowledged in succession as chief-mistresses: the good-natured, empty-headed Louise de la Vallière, the clever, scheming Françoise-Athenais de Montespan and the bossy, prudish Françoise de Maintenon. Each mistress was older than her predecessor and came to the king's attention while a member of her predecessor's entourage. As we have seen, Louis' infidelities distressed the queen who nevertheless regretted the kindly Louise de la Vallière's exile to a nunnery, for she infinitely preferred her to her horrid successor. Madame de Maintenon persuaded Louis to be nice to the queen. After Maria Theresa's death in 1683, Louis married Madame de Maintenon and under her dour influence he had no more extra-marital adventures.

Although Louis XIV rewarded his mistresses materially, his relations with women show him at his most egocentric. Typical was his behaviour in 1667 when he obliged his ladies to go campaigning with him in Flanders. The royal coach contained the king, the queen, Louise de la Vallière, who was on her way out, and Madame de Montespan, who was very much on her way in. It was, as can be imagined, not exactly a jolly company. Louis did not improve matters by refusing to stop for anyone else's calls of nature; furthermore he was highly offended if the ladies declined his frequent offers of vast quantities of food. The heat was suffocating and the roads were atrocious, especially for Louise who was pregnant. Louis himself remained in excellent spirits. In fact he was the life and soul of the party, for he adored campaigns.

Louis was furious if his current mistress was unavailable, implicitly taking the line that periods and pregnancies occurred specially to inconvenience him. When it was reported that one of his mistresses had miscarried, Louis was delighted, for she would soon be back in his bed again. Even de Maintenon found Louis very difficult and demanding. She asked her confessor if she really had to submit to sex twice a night (they were both over seventy) and she suffered from Louis' insistence on all the windows being open, whatever the time of year. Although there is no record of Louis XIV forcing a woman to sleep with him - and this claim cannot be made for his fellow royal lecher, Charles II - the picture which emerges is of an utter male-chauvinist.

But then he was the king. There is a revealing anecdote about his conduct as an infant at the death of Louis XIII in 1643, when he had just been christened. 'What name did they give you?' asked the dying king. 'I'm Louis XIV'. 'No, not yet', whispered his father. If the Sun King strikes us as being egocentric, it must be remembered that from his very birth he was literally at the centre of the stage.

Did he have any relationships with people who could criticise him to his face or answer him back? Certainly not his only legitimate son, 'Monseigneur', the Dauphin (1661-1711). He was a heavy, stupid man who took after his mother and was terrified of his father. Certainly not the king's ministers. There was only his brother, Philippe - for Louis XIII and Anne of Austria produced another 'miracle child'.

Philippe has had a bad press. 'Monsieur', as the king's brother was called, has been condemned for his treatment of Charles II's sister Minette, his first wife, contriving to be both a jealous husband and a homosexual. Otherwise historians have tended not to take this scented little Bourbon prince seriously. Be-ribboned, frivolous, selfish, on the face of it Philippe compares badly with his imposing brother. Yet there are grounds both for sympathising with Philippe and for admiring him. He was handled neither generously nor perceptively by the Sun King who consistently under-rated his brother's loyalty. In order to prevent him becoming another Gaston, he was deprived of influence and responsibility and treated with patronising condescension: 'Brother, go and amuse yourself - we're going to take counsel'. When Philippe won the battle of Cassel in 1678, Louis was furious and never allowed him to command an army again. Philippe reacted to this dismissive treatment by occasionally telling Louis some home truths. While growing up together the two princes had quarrelled as brothers will do, once throwing soup all over each other, on another occasion urinating on each other's beds. They occasionally quarrelled as adults - for instance, when Louis reprimanded his brother for preferring boy-friends to his wife. 'If it's a matter of correcting faults, what about yours?' Monsieur shouted at the king. 'Mine are with women, yours are an abominable vice', Louis smugly retorted. It was after a furious row over Louis' unfair treatment of Philippe's son, the duc de Chartres, that Philippe had a fatal apoplectic fit in 1701; Louis was devastated with remorse.

No-one else dared speak bluntly to Louis XIV. Flattered by courtiers and always the centre of attention, what chance had he of being modest or self-critical? It is amazing that he was as likeable as he was and that he did not indulge himself more. Apart from his sexual liaisons, Louis' only other vice was gluttony - and this may have been caused by his doctors' inability to cure his tape-worms; he was always hungry. Courteous, affable and charming, Louis XIV was well-suited to rule a court. Whether he could rule a country is another matter.

Making notes on *Introduction: the Study of Louis XIV*

It would be a most unusual exam paper on seventeenth and eighteenth-century Europe which did not contain questions on Louis XIV's reign. Careful and methodical note-taking are therefore likely to produce dividends in the exam room. The following controversial issues certainly attract examiners: i) Louis XIV's system of government, ii) his achievements as ruler of France, with especial emphasis on the economy and on religion, iii) his foreign policy and wars, and iv) an assessment of his merits and achievements as a ruler and his greatness as a king.

All these issues will be tackled thoroughly in the chapters devoted to them (see the table of contents). Likewise the Conclusion contains a discussion of Louis XIV's record, his merits and demerits. It would be best to postpone detailed note-taking on these issues until you study the relevant chapters.

Even so a brief summary of the controversial aspects of the reign could with profit be made at this stage. It would help you to remember what you should be looking for as you embark on your study of Louis XIV. You will be able to use this summary as a checklist when you have finished your initial reading of this book to ensure that you have done the job properly. Also, it is likely that you will enjoy your study more if you are fully aware of the questions to which you should be finding answers.

It is my hope that you will find the section on the Sun King's background and personality easy reading and that the picture presented to you will be remembered. Therefore, detailed notes should not really be necessary on this section. Provided that you have a clear idea in your mind of the sort of man we are dealing with when we study Louis XIV's reign, the more complicated aspects of the story (which are discussed in later chapters) should fall into place readily.

Nevertheless, you might find it helpful to draw up a brief list of those of Louis' qualities and defects which you think are relevant to his performance as king of France and were major influences on his development both as a ruler and as a human being. The Introduction ends with the question, 'Could Louis XIV rule a country as well as a court?'. Why not make your own 'educated guess' as to how successful he was likely to be, using the information which you now have about what made him tick?

CHAPTER 2

The Politics of Absolutism

1 Absolutism: Definition and Implications

In the Introduction we established that the Sun King *mattered*. Louis
XIV's role as King of France was so central and so crucial that his
strengths and weaknesses, his virtues and vices were bound to make a
difference for good or ill. However, Louis mattered not only because he
was the king but also because of the *way* he reigned. For he established a
formidable reputation as a masterful ruler, as the classic example of
absolute monarchy in action. In this chapter we shall examine the ways
in which Louis made his mark, beginning with the concept of absolutism
which gave Louis XIV's kingship its style.

What is meant by the description of Louis XIV as an 'absolute
monarch'? The derivation of 'absolute' is that a ruler is 'absolved' from
subordination to any human authority. Unlike contemporary kings of
England, Louis was able to choose his policies and his ministers without
looking over his shoulder at parliament. He was not required to consult
his subjects, but could take decisions promptly and implement them
forcefully. Nor did he have to justify his actions or listen to criticism. He
could demand unquestioning obedience.

However, some historians suggest that this picture is more theoretical
than real. In practice Louis' power was limited, as was the power of any
seventeenth-century ruler. He was limited by the moral conventions of
the age such as the contemporary disapproval of political assassination
and of mass murder. He was limited by his lack of repressive institutions
such as a secret police. The Russian dictator Joseph Stalin was described
as 'Genghis Khan with a telephone'. Louis XIV lacked both Stalin's
unscrupulousness and his telephone.

Nevertheless contemporaries certainly regarded Louis XIV as an
absolute king; indeed the French admired him for being absolute. The
denial of individual liberty which absolutism implies may repel
twentieth-century liberals. Yet to many seventeenth-century thinkers
absolutism seemed not only the most efficient but also the most
enlightened way of ruling a state. An instructive parallel is the high
regard right-wing people had for fascism in the 1920s and 1930s; a
no-nonsense approach seemed the best way to get things done.

Not that the French equated absolutism with tyranny. On the
contrary, everyone from the king downwards believed that a Christian
ruler however absolute had overriding duties both to God and his
subjects. As the father of his people he should behave responsibly,
remembering that although he had no constitutional obligation to keep
the law, the law still existed, and that it was a Christian king's duty to
uphold its authority. Bourbon absolutism had been established by Louis
XIV's grandfather Henri IV who deferred to nobody, and yet showed

concern for all his subjects. Louis XIV himself resented the picture which his enemies painted of him as an arbitrary tyrant. Such had been Herod who slew the Holy Innocents; such was reputed to be the Turkish Sultan who had men beheaded at his personal whim. The Most Christian King, as the King of France was traditionally styled, would not act like that.

In this chapter you will be invited to come to your own conclusions about whether Louis XIV was a tyrant, whether he was efficient, and whether he was successful in solving his problems. We shall look critically at the system of government which he inherited and at the ways in which he developed it. What was distinctive about his style of absolutism? What did his absolutism amount to in practice? We shall begin by asking why Louis chose absolutism as the way forward in 1661.

2 The Case for Absolutism

Absolutism was an attractive option for Louis XIV when his personal rule began in 1661. France was such a big place. In those days it took a man a fortnight to get from Paris to the Mediterranean. Given the lack of modern telecommunications, this was the only way for correspondence to reach its destination - that is to say, as fast and no faster than a horse could carry a man. So it was hard for the government of such a large country to acquire up-to-date information or issue prompt orders. It was even harder actually to enforce instructions. When you are sitting in an office at Versailles how do you impose an edict 500 miles away? How do you lay hands on a defiant and popular rebel? How do you collect taxation from impoverished and discontented peasants? How do you suppress an armed revolt without the operation taking months if not years?

These questions are especially relevant when we consider the historical background to Louis XIV's personal rule. Louis' grandfather Henri IV (1589-1610) inherited a troubled throne. The stability of France had been undermined for thirty years by royal minorities and weak kings, overmighty nobles, foreign invasion and religious strife. Henri IV initiated a recovery of royal authority; but he was assassinated before he could achieve a permanent settlement of the crown's problems. His son and Louis XIV's father, Louis XIII (1610-43), eventually established his own authority, aided by his chief minister Cardinal Richelieu. But Louis XIII's death ushered in another minority. The attempts of a second chief minister wearing a cardinal's hat, the unpopular Italian Jules Mazarin, to maintain the authority of the crown caused the revolts known as the *Frondes* (1649-53). While the *Frondes* were disrupting France, across the Channel the English political nation executed its king and made England a republic - developments which Frenchmen watched with interest. In the event the French monarchy survived - but only with difficulty.

As we have seen in chapter 1, Louis was profoundly influenced by the *Frondes*. He never forgot being hustled out of palaces in the middle of the night to avoid being kidnapped. He saw his mother humiliated by ambitious nobles, some of them his own flesh and blood. He saw Mazarin chased out of the country. He was aware that the royal family and the chief minister were lampooned in scurrilous rhymes. Royal power was questioned by insolent lawyers in the *parlement* of Paris. Above all, France was reduced to the chaos of civil war. The private armies of the nobility leagued with France's enemies the Spanish. Louis retained to his life's end a concern for order, authority and national security as a result of the nightmare which he had to endure as a child-king.

Nor had Mazarin totally restored the situation by his death in 1661. Certainly the cardinal had crowned his diplomatic career by arranging the peace of the Pyrenees which concluded a century of war between France and Spain to France's advantage. Certainly he had rebuilt a capable team of royal administrators. Certainly he had made his own fortune - 'That I should have to leave all this!' were his dying words as he wistfully surveyed his pictures. But he had left the crown in debt, the administration encumbered with 40,000 hereditary office-holders who should not be confused with the professional civil service of a modern state, and the country impoverished and discontented.

Given, therefore, the difficulties involved in governing so large a country as France combined with the historical background in 1661, was there not a case for absolutism? Indeed, were there alternatives? Would it have made sense to dismantle the governmental machinery which Louis inherited and cancel royal absolutism by introducing representative rule? Not even the leaders of the *Frondes* had suggested alternatives to authoritarian monarchy; they had merely proved the case for absolutism by their selfish irresponsibility. Nobody wanted a renewal of chaos and violence. Louis XIV and the vast majority of his contemporaries believed that even a tyrant was preferable to the collapse of law and order. So there was a strong case for Louis XIV to adopt a firm, reasonable, absolutist approach.

3 Absolutism Confirmed, 1661

It could be argued therefore that when Mazarin died the question was not whether absolutism would be maintained but what sort of absolutism there would be. Louis XIV inherited both the tradition and the machinery of absolutism, with the men to serve him. What use did he make of these assets and how did he mould them to suit his purposes?

Louis XIV appreciated that if he was indeed to be an absolute king, there was no substitute for having direct, personal control of the government. This was his greatest claim to originality, for France had been ruled for half a century by chief ministers acting on behalf of the

Crown. Louis was determined to put an end to a system which threatened to undermine his own absolutist role. He would be the managing director as well as the chairman of the board!

On 10 March 1661, the day after Mazarin died, Louis XIV summoned the men who had ruled France under the leadership of the late chief minister: Le Tellier who had reformed the army, Fouquet, the brilliant and dangerously ambitious Superintendant of Finances, Seguier the Chancellor, and Brienne and Lionne who between them had run foreign affairs. The 22-year-old king coolly surveyed these experienced, capable, middle-aged statesmen who in their turn assessed their young master, wondering which of them he would choose to succeed the cardinal as his chief minister. Then the king exploded his bombshell. Addressing the Chancellor, he said:

1 Monsieur, I have called you, together with my secretaries and ministers of state, to tell you that up to this moment I have been pleased to entrust the government of my affairs to the late Cardinal. It is now time that I govern them myself. You will assist
5 me with your counsels when I ask for them. Outside of the regular business of justice which I do not intend to change, Monsieur the Chancellor, I request and order you to seal no orders except by my command, or after having discussed them with me, or at least not unless a secretary brings them to you on my behalf. And you,
10 Messieurs, my secretaries of state, I order you not to sign anything, not even a passport, without my command; to render account to me personally each day and to favour no one.

Soon afterwards the president of the assembly of the clergy who had previously liaised with Mazarin asked the king to whom he should report in future; 'To me, Archbishop, to me', Louis replied.

Fouquet unwisely broadcast his opinion that Louis should not be taken seriously. Others doubted whether the young man would really handle all the government business himself; surely he would get bored with such trivialities as passports and would return to his soldiers and his mistresses, perhaps reserving for himself the major decisions. But the sceptics were wrong. People often take after their grandparents; Louis resembled his great-grandfather Philip II of Spain who had been meticulous in discharging administrative duties. For the next 54 years the Sun King really was his own chief minister.

Given Louis XIV's determination to control affairs himself, how did he go about making his will effective? To answer this question, we must assess the system of government which he inherited and the use which he made of it. For Louis was a conservative administrator, achieving results by development and adaptation rather than by innovation. So what was at his disposal when he took over the controls?

In 1661 the royal system of government was conciliar; that is to say,

Anne of Austria and Mazarin had consulted their councillors, involving them in decision-making and in putting those decisions into practice. Similarly, Louis XIV always respected the expert opinion of the men who comprised his council and carefully listened to them. Just how influential they were remains to be seen; but they were regularly required to express their thoughts and to co-operate in government.

Nobody was a member of the royal council by right. The king summoned men whose opinions he valued or whom he wished to honour. Louis XIV copied Mazarin by excluding royal princes, members of the high nobility and prominent churchmen. However historians who claim that Louis favoured middle-class administrators are wrong, paying too much attention to the memoirs of that aristocratic snob, the duc de Saint-Simon. Louis XIV was a snob too; he would not have dreamt of employing plebeian councillors and sure enough all his appointments were members of at least the lesser nobility.

The chief administrators at the centre of government were the Chancellor, the Controller-General and the Secretaries of State. The Chancellor was responsible for issuing royal edicts and for supervising the legal system. The Controller-General was the chief financial officer. There were four Secretaries of State, the first responsible for war, the second for the royal household, Paris, the clergy and the navy, the third for foreign affairs, and the fourth for Protestant affairs. All these men were directly answerable to the king. They were of course supported by assistants. What is astonishing, however, is that so much was achieved by so few. It has been calculated that Louis XIV's government at its most bureaucratic was manned by only about a thousand administrators. They must have taken their cue from the king and worked very hard indeed.

Whether the government's policies were in fact implemented depended on the co-operation of officials throughout the length and breadth of France. Local government in Louis XIV's time was a mixture of corruption, moral blackmail and genuine public service. Most office-holders inherited their positions in return for a cash payment; this extraordinary practice had been officially recognised by Henri IV and was known as the *paulette* (after Paulet the first collector of the payment). To an increasing extent, however, office-holders were first-time buyers of posts which had been dreamt up by the Crown in order to raise money. Office-holders expected a return on their investment; their salary for doing the job would be supplemented by bribes from people for whom they could do favours. Ever-increasing graft gave birth to ever-increasing inefficiency as the Crown created more and more posts, not because they were needed but in order to sell them for short-term gains. How could such a 'system' work?

From Louis XIV's point of view the crucial issue was the raising and collecting of taxation. If he was to execute his foreign policy and cut a figure as a prestigious monarch, he needed cash. How was taxation raised? In some parts of France known as *pays d'états* the local estates negotiated with the representatives of the Crown in order to establish what should be the total tax revenue. The estates would then raise the money as best they could. In the *pays d'élection* on the other hand the government had more direct control; taxes were collected in theory by government agents, in practice by syndicates of tax farmers. It was not an efficient system. No doubt some of the excuses for meagre results were genuine, while some were not: people were too poor to be able to pay due to a recent famine, the tax-collectors had been robbed by highwaymen, the money had certainly been dispatched and its non-arrival was therefore a total mystery. It was in order to sort out such problems that seventeenth-century French governments developed their administrative trump-card - the *intendant.*

There were sixteenth-century precedents for these government trouble-shooters. Richelieu extended their responsibilities and powers using them not only to extract taxation for his expensive foreign policy but also to discipline troops, organise supplies, keep streets clean, monitor the price of food and impose the death penalty in the law-courts. *Intendants* served for a limited amount of time in their *generalités,* as their administrative areas were called - usually for three years. Normally they had no family or financial connection with their *generalités.* They did not buy their office and they could be dismissed by the Crown without any repercussions. There were 31 *intendants* when Louis XIV's personal rule began.

It used to be thought that *intendants* represented the Crown's policy of increasing its own power at the expense of more traditional authorities such as provincial governors and the local aristocracy. However, this view has been modified by recent research. Scholars now stress the co-operation between *intendants* and provincial governors; they supported and complemented each other's authority. Indeed it was the weakness of provincial governors rather than their strength which prompted the Crown to develop the role of the *intendant.* Nor did Louis XIV or his predecessors relish conflict with the nobility; compromise not confrontation was the goal. It is true that the leaders of the *Frondes* demanded the withdrawal of the *intendants,* and that Mazarin temporarily complied with this demand. But the target here was the taxes which the *intendants* were collecting rather than the wish to get rid of the *intendants* as such. By 1661 the *intendants* were back, though they were instructed to adopt a low profile, to co-operate with the local élites and wherever possible to avoid confrontation.

If there was resentment against the *intendants* it came from the *parlements.* These were royal courts where the *noblesse de robe* (the lesser nobles who had made their career in the law as opposed to the army) exercised their authority. These aristocratic lawyers treasured their rights to register the laws of the land, settle legal disputes and pronounce on disputed financial issues. Not surprisingly they recognised the *intendants* as a threat to their powers and privileges for which in many instances they had paid good money.

It is clear that Louis XIV inherited a machinery of government which had definitely worked after a fashion under his predecessors. From the point of view of an ambitious, masterful, absolutist king, there was a lot wrong with it. It was cumbersome and limited by distance, poverty and lack of reliable and trained administrators. But it was there, ready to function and open to development by a strong monarch.

4 The Development of the System by Louis XIV

Louis XIV may have been a conservative administrator, but his determination to be master, to put absolutist theory into practice, prompted him to innovate when it suited his interests. For instance royal government became more bureaucratic and centralised. In 1682 all departments accompanied the court to the palace of Versailles which now became the administrative hub of the Sun King's absolutist empire. From a practical point of view the new set-up was an improvement on the previous haphazard distribution of offices round Paris.

How effective were Louis XIV's alterations to the system which he had inherited? Historians have been most favourably impressed by the first 11 years of the personal rule (1661-72) emphasising how constructive this period was and giving much of the credit to the remarkable Jean-Baptiste Colbert. This is fair enough provided that we remember that there was life after Colbert and that he was but one member of a capable team dominated by the king. Furthermore, by no means all Colbert's initiatives achieved their purposes, nor were his successors men of straw with no achievements to their credit.

The team which Louis inherited from Mazarin certainly combined ability with experience. The three ministers who were the members of the inner council during these years were known as the Triad: Colbert, Le Tellier and Lionne. Le Tellier, ably assisted by his son Louvois, concentrated on military reform, Lionne specialised in foreign affairs and Colbert in virtually everything else. After the disgrace of Fouquet in 1664 (see page 56) the post of Superintendant of Finances was abolished. Colbert became Superintendant of the King's Buildings (1664), Controller-General of Finances (1665), and Secretary of State for the Navy (1669). He is best known for his direction of the French economy (see page 58). But Colbert's achievements as a patron of the arts were also remarkable (see page 82) and he was the most prominent of the Triad in developing the effectiveness of royal government.

What changes occurred during the personal rule? 'Not that many', according to some historians; continuity rather than revolution was the order of the day. Even so there were significant developments. We have already identified Louis' determination to be his own chief minister and the increasing size and professionalism of the royal bureaucracy. Taking the reign as a whole, we can identify three particular areas in which Louis XIV's kingship became more absolute.

a) The Law

The law posed crucial questions for an absolute king. Was his power limited by the necessity of respecting his subjects' legal rights? Did the king need the co-operation of the *parlements* in order to legislate? So far as Louis XIV was concerned, a particularly acute problem was France's legal profession, with its jealously guarded privileges. Such issues would test the young king's astuteness.

Straight away Louis XIV reduced the legal profession's influence in favour of careerist royal administrators. For example, the most influential royal bureaucrat had hitherto been the Chancellor, the realm's senior law official who often deputised for the king in the courts. However, Louis engineered the replacement of the Chancellor by the Controller-General as the key figure in the government. Indeed it was Colbert the Controller-General who proceeded to reform the law; not even in his own sphere of activity did the Chancellor make the running. Backed by the king, Colbert introduced the civil code (1667), the criminal code (1670), the maritime code (1672), and the commercial code (1673). After Colbert's death the black code (1685) clarified the rights of slaves in French colonies. The purpose of these codes was to speed up the various legal processes; the civil code standardised the procedures for summonses, trials and retrials. The *parlement* of Paris was certainly consulted, but Louis was also advised by a council of justice set up in 1665, dominated by Colbert. After due deliberation Louis himself acted in his role as absolute law-giver of the realm.

Various measures were taken in order to diminish the authority of the *parlements*. It was established in 1661 that the royal council's decrees had precedence over those of the *parlements*. In 1665 the *parlements* were called 'superior' rather than 'sovereign' courts. From 1673 the *parlement* of Paris had to register royal edicts at once and could only remonstrate when it had done so; the fact that this measure was discussed with the *parlement's* leaders beforehand did not detract from its significance, for the *parlement* had now lost its control over legislation. Here again we have absolutism in action.

Louis XIV now methodically exploited his hold over the legal profession. Lawyers staffed a royal inquiry into the conduct of irresponsible nobles in the Auvergne; brutal exploitation of the peasantry was brought to light and the perpetrators disciplined. In 1665 at Louis' instigation the *parlement* of Paris investigated the ancestry of allegedly noble families; several nobles had to solicit the support of their local *intendant* to prove their credentials. The king's control over the Church was increased by the extension of the *régale* - the appropriation of the revenues of a vacant bishopric; this royal privilege had formerly applied only in certain dioceses, but now it was extended by the king's lawyers to the whole realm. The campaign to achieve religious unity through the persecution of the Huguenots (see page 37) was orchestrated by the king's lawyers, culminating in the revocation of the Edict of Nantes. Similarly the lawyers were on hand to support Louis' acquisitive foreign policy (see page 99).

Were there any limitations on the king's power to exploit the law? There was a significant test case at the very end of the reign. Tragically the court doctors had killed all Louis XIV's legitimate heirs except his infant great-grandson, the duc d'Anjou. Louis was not to know that this little boy would not only succeed him as Louis XV but would live to the age of sixty-four. The Sun King therefore decided that if Anjou were to die young, his own bastards were to be eligible for the succession. A royal edict of July 1714 declared that 'M. the duc du Maine and M. the comte de Toulouse and their male descendants, there being no princes of royal blood' may succeed to the throne. While the king and Madame de Maintenon were devoted to these two sons whom Madame de Montespan had borne him, Louis' chief preoccupation was concern for the succession. But the royal edict was in flagrant defiance of the law of the land and the Church's law both of which denied a bastard's right to succeed. The legitimate heir if the duc d'Anjou were to die was the king's nephew the duc d'Orleans. Actually Louis and Madame de Maintenon hated and despised Orleans; and they may have had some cause to believe that he would be a disaster as king. Did this justify Louis XIV's open defiance of the law?

The *parlement* of Paris dutifully registered the edict of July 1714 and a month later formally received Maine and Toulouse as princes of the blood. The king reiterated his decision by making a will in which he denied Orleans his right to be regent in favour of a council including Maine and Toulouse; he deposited this will with the *parlement*. In the event the will was simply ignored after Louis XIV's death when Orleans became sole regent in accordance with law and custom. The Sun King's attempt to re-write the law with regard to the succession had failed.

Although the *parlement* reluctantly condoned Louis' attempts to flout the law of succession, there was open defiance of the king when he tried to impose the papal bull *Unigenitus* on France in September 1713. This bull represented the alliance of pope and king to suppress Jansenism (see page 43); it conflicted with the Gallican Articles of 1682. The *parlement* of Paris refused to register *Unigenitus* until the bishops had approved it - which they were clearly reluctant to do. In the end *parlement* accepted the bull with reservations and refused to prosecute bishops who had led clerical opposition. Some provincial *parlements* also dared to oppose the bull.

Do Louis XIV's ineffectual attempts to legitimise his bastards and to impose *Unigenitus* suggest that his ability to ride roughshod over the law was limited? Certainly Louis was prepared to compromise. His use of *lits de justice* which enabled him to overrule *parlements* and of *lettres de cachet* which permitted him to arrest people without going through the courts was cautious. He obtained the approval of the *parlement* of Paris before introducing the *dixième* in 1710; this was a tax on income which strictly speaking contravened the laws granting immunity to privileged classes. All in all Louis himself accepted the contemporary view that only a tyrant ignored the existence of the law; for most of the time he did his best to behave 'legally'.

However, we are left with the overriding impression of a clever and masterful ruler who increased his own power by manipulating his legal rights and exploiting to his own profit the ambitions of the lawyers. Here was a significant and successful development of royal absolutism.

b) The Army

A crucial area for the exercise of royal absolutism was the army. Traditionally the King of France's authority depended on his ability to lead his fellow soldiers into battle. Both Louis' grandfather Henri IV and his father Louis XIII had fulfilled this role. However, both kings had from time to time experienced the disloyalty and unreliability of their own military subordinates who had conspired against the Crown with foreign foes or with each other. Furthermore the rank and file, the 'licentious soldiery', were a perpetual headache to the authorities. Nevertheless, the soldiers and their leaders were traditionally the king's army and if capably handled could be more of an asset than a liability to their royal master.

Louis XIV dominated his armies through sheer professionalism. He won the respect of his soldiers from the highest ranks to the lowest by demonstrating his own ability as a soldier. For much of the reign Louis had to play the role of a supreme commander, co-ordinating his armies from royal headquarters; as we shall see, he did this with authority and determination. However, he quite often led his troops in battle himself, for example during the Dutch war where he proved to be a capable strategist. He was at his best in directing sieges where he showed himself to be resourceful and shrewd. He won his soldiers' gratitude as an organiser and administrator, establishing the Invalides hospital in Paris for wounded and retired soldiers. Louis' involvement in military affairs came naturally to him. He cared deeply about his troops' welfare. He was genuinely interested in military affairs, invariably well-informed and perceptive. He enjoyed war, was physically brave and readily took to camp life. He was happy among his soldiers, while they responded by welcoming him enthusiastically; the army's morale improved when Louis led in person.

However, the paramount reason for Louis XIV's success in dominating his armies was the establishment of his authority over the officer corps. This was partly the result of the Sun King's effective campaign to control and tame France's aristocracy, to which we shall turn later in this chapter; for senior commanders were almost invariably noblemen of the sword. But Louis also owed his success to unspectacular attention to detail. This quality is well illustrated by his control over appointments. Not only were senior commanders the king's choices, for Louis established his right to appoint every officer down to the rank of colonel. It was a royal army; the king decreed who commanded, who was promoted, who was demoted.

Louis' right-hand man in the imposition of absolutist control over the army was Francois-Michel Le Tellier, marquis de Louvois, (known to historians as Louvois). This formidable and abrasive administrator had been trained by his father, Michel Le Tellier, who had directed military affairs under Mazarin and during the first decade of the personal rule. Louvois inherited his father's organisational skills, as he showed by developing *magazins* which were centres for supplying the armies with food and equipment. Regularly paid and fed, the soldiers became more reliable and better disciplined. Louvois' particular contribution was to increase centralised direction of France's armies. Gone were the days when army commanders were independent agents owing only theoretical loyalty to their distant king. Gradually - it did not happen overnight - Louvois was able to insist on the king's generals accepting direction from the king himself and from his war secretary .

Louvois has had a bad press, both from contemporaries and from historians: 'this horrible man', Nancy Mitford calls him. He has been blamed for war-time atrocities such as the devastation of the Palatinate (see page 116) and such crimes against humanity as the persecution of the Huguenots. On the other hand, recent historians have emphasised Louvois' loyalty and efficiency; his sharpening up of the postal service for example made centralised bureaucracy more effective. But Louvois was no psychologist; his handling of such *prima donnas* as Condé and Turenne was tactless, and the needlessly bossy approach he adopted was understandably resented. Madame de Sévigné gave us this picture of Louvois rebuking an aristocratic courtier:

1 Monsieur de Louvois said the other day to Monsieur de Nogaret: 'Sir, your company is in a very poor state.' 'I did not know that, Sir,' replied Nogaret. 'Then Sir, you should have known it,' retorted Louvois, 'Have you seen your company?' 'No Sir.' 'Then 5 you should have done so, Sir. You must choose, Sir, either to be an avowed courtier, or to perform your duties if you are going to be an officer.'

But the main cause of Louvois' unpopularity was the policy which he carried out on his master's behalf. The subordination of army commanders to central control can rightly be seen as a prime example of a general tendency towards absolutism - the invasion of the individual's independence by royal bureaucracy. Inevitably this process caused resentment; Louis benefited while Louvois took the rap.

For here we have the classic demonstration of royal absolutism as practised by Louis XIV. He established the principle that war was too important, too complex, and too expensive to be left to generals, and that armies were too dangerous a threat to the Crown to be controlled by their commanders. So the king reduced the status of France's generals. The logical conclusion came after Louvois' death in 1691. Officially Louvois was succeeded by his son Barbezieux, but in effect Louis became his own war minister. His control of the army was now all-pervasive.

c) Control of Local Government from the Centre

To a great extent local government presented Louis XIV with no problems. For centuries the aristocracy had administered both the countryside and the towns. They had been supplemented by an influx of salaried office-holders during the century preceding Louis' personal rule. In theory all these officials, from the aristocratic governor of a province downwards, were the king's men who could be left to get on with the job. There was little threat to Louis XIV's absolutism here, for a basic community of interest existed between the king and the governing classes. Occasionally, seventeenth-century defiance of the Crown involved all sectors of society. For most of the time, however, the ruling class agreed with the king that such causes of public disorder as starving peasants, out-of-work artisans, discharged soldiers and homeless vagrants should be kept down or locked up.

Nevertheless, throughout his reign, but particularly under Colbert's influence, Louis XIV intervened in local government. As we have seen, this was for one reason: to raise more money in taxation. Louis' foreign policy and his building projects were expensive. Colbert's job was to provide the financial resources for them. The money came from the French people, who were understandably reluctant to pay. The extraction of this money therefore became a priority for Colbert, on his master's behalf; hence royal involvement in local government. This was achieved by increasing the authority and the responsibilities of the *intendants*. The formidable Controller-General presided over the whole administrative structure from the centre.

By studying Colbert's methods and by examining his achievements, much can be learned about royal absolutism in action. We can discover its strengths and weaknesses, and the ways in which success could be achieved. It is worth looking over the great minister's shoulder.

Colbert was a typical bureaucrat. Charged with the raising of money, his first priority was to gather up-to-date, accurate information. His special representatives, the *intendants*, were first and foremost Colbert's eyes and ears. They had to select the right compromise between excessive attention to detail on the one hand and superficiality on the other. Here is Colbert laying down the law in 1682 to Foucault, his *intendant* at Montauban:

> 1 I have submitted a report to the king about the memoir you have
> sent me, describing your inspection of your generality; but as you
> have not given an account of your tour election by election [an
> 'election' was an administrative district], and have produced a
> 5 general survey instead, His Majesty is not satisfied with it, because
> it was his intention that you should visit each election in your
> generality, allowing yourself plenty of time to do so, and should
> inform him in detail of your findings.

Here, by way of contrast, is Colbert's criticism of Marle, the *intendant* at Riom (23 September 1672):

> 1 It seems that I must say to you once more that you are much too
> eager to order general investigations during the course of your
> work, and that these large-scale enquiries serve only to vex the
> people, forcing them to come from the farthest corners of the
> 5 generality in order for them to bring their papers to your office,
> thus loading you with endless amounts of documents.

However vital up-to-date information was, the actual raising of money from the localities often depended on the influence of local governors and bishops rather than *intendants*. This was especially the case in the *pays d'états* where taxes were agreed by the Estates. In June 1662 the duc de Bourbon, Governor of Burgundy, reported to Colbert:

> 1 The Estates have had discussions every day, and the extreme
> misery from which the province is suffering, whether it is because
> of the heavy burdens they have shouldered in the past, or the recent
> years of dearth, or the disorders which have been creeping steadily
> 5 forward for some time, has convinced them that His Majesty will
> give them some relief on this occasion. This is why they came to me
> the first time with an offer of only 500,000 livres for the free gift.
> Then, after I had told them what I thought of that, they raised it to
> 600,then 800, and finally to 900,000. Until then I had been
> 10 resolutely insisting on 1,500,000; but I realised at that moment
> that they had almost certainly decided not to give any more. I
> therefore reduced it to 1,200,000.

The duc de Bourbon and the Estates of Burgundy finally agreed on 1,000,000 livres. Lest it be thought that such a Dutch auction was unbecoming for an aristocrat, we find a prince of the Church involved in similar haggling with the Estates of Province in 1671. The Bishop of Marseille told Colbert how the Estates began by offering a mere 200,000 livres in response to the king's demand for 500,000; would Colbert suggest to His Majesty that he would be lucky to get 450,000?

When it came to raising money from the towns, the greatest problem was that only too often the municipal authorities were hopelessly in debt - either due to borrowing in order to pay previous years' taxes, or because of unnecessary prestigious building or thanks to grossly extravagant expenses claimed by town officials. It was obviously essential to ensure that mayors and their deputies were reliable and capable. We therefore find Colbert in correspondence with the local bishops. Thus Colbert to the Bishop of Auxerre (10 February 1672):

1 Monseigneur le Duc de Bourbon keeps pressing me to tell him the men whom I consider to be the most suitable for the posts of mayor and consuls of Auxerre; and as I know no one who is more concerned than you that worthy men be selected, I ask you to send me your thoughts on the subject. But it is vital that this be kept
6 secret.

While badly-managed municipalities might have difficulty in paying their share, the most persistent problem was rural poverty. The cruel paradox that the poorest members of society, the peasants, had to pay most, was ubiquitous in Bourbon France. Colbert's missive of 1662 to La Barré, *intendant* at Riom, speaks for itself:

1 The king has received a number of complaints that, during the weeks of the harvest, troops have been used to aid the collection of taxes in your generality, thus causing widespread disorder and bringing great hardship to the people, who have already suffered a
5 bad year. I have firmly assured His Majesty that you will quickly remedy this situation, and that, in the months of July and August, you will not allow anyone to exert pressure of any kind on the parishes, because it is only reasonable to give them time to bring in the harvest so that they may afterwards be in a position to acquit
10 themselves of their obligations.

Colbert's priorities are significant. Similarly he had to insist again and again that peasants' livestock should not be confiscated in lieu of unpaid tax; for what was the sense in totally ruining the taxpayer of the future by depriving his ground of manure? Equally grim is the frequent reference to tax collectors being beaten up or imprisoned by desperate countryfolk. This must not happen, insisted Colbert, and those responsible must be brought to justice. Colbert displayed similar realism in rejecting excuses for nonpayment of taxes. He counselled the *intendant* at Orleans to be sceptical about the alleged damage wrought by severe hailstorms; 'you must remember that the fuss which is made about these storms is often greater than their actual effect'. Similarly tax exemption for the fathers of ten or more children must not be granted where the children have died.

Colbert and his successors laboured indefatigably to collect the taxes to which the king was entitled. It is an unattractive story of deals between selfish élites, of dishonesty, cynicism and force (there were occasions when Colbert sanctioned the employment of troops). However, the over-riding impression is not one of tyranny but of compromise. Louis XIV achieved co-operation by making concessions, granting privileges and accepting half a loaf when he might have hoped for more. Colbert, the king's estate manager, achieved success as a fixer rather than as a bully. This was absolutism by negotiation.

But what success! Nothing illustrates the increasing effectiveness of Louis XIV's absolutism better than the astonishing amounts of money raised through taxation, especially towards the end of the reign. Colbert's successors Pontchartrain and Desmarets, employing and developing his techniques, were able to finance the cripplingly expensive wars which lasted from 1688 to 1713. Not only did revenue increase considerably beyond the high levels already achieved under Richelieu and Mazarin, but the regularity and relative ease with which these vast sums were collected are highly significant and indicative of the sheer power of royal absolutism.

5 The Essential Features of Louis XIV's Kingship

We have seen how successful Louis XIV was in developing the absolutist state in a number of key areas. To what extent did the credit for these achievements belong to Louis personally, and how far should it be shared with able ministers such as Colbert? What was Louis XIV like as a decision-maker, as a team-leader, as a man-manager? Was the secret of his success his own approach to his job - if you like, his distinctive style of government? Did Louis' brand of personal absolutism suit the demands of ruling late-seventeenth-century France?

The most impressive characteristic of Louis XIV's style was his devotion to the job. This was based on his own self-identification with France. Perhaps Louis XIV never said *'l'état c'est moi'* ('I am the state') - his most celebrated 'quote' - although on his deathbed he did say 'the king dies but the state is immortal'. Both remarks reflect the Sun King's political philosophy. He saw himself as the embodiment of the state, but at the same time its servant. There were great dangers in such a close identification of France with himself. On occasions he confused the welfare of the French people with his own prestige or with the interests of the Bourbon dynasty. But there were positive aspects as well. In particular Louis' professionalism, his devotion to duty and his sheer determination to triumph over adversity must command respect. Once when he was tormented with pain caused by an anal fistula it was suggested to him that he could with a good conscience miss the customary daily *lévèr* (when the king got dressed in public, formally attended by his nobles) but Louis replied, 'We are not private persons, we owe ourselves to the public'.

Louis XIV's exercise of personal responsibility for the government of a great nation for 54 years is astonishing. In fact, it is an all-time record. The nearest comparable contenders are Elizabeth I of England who reigned for 45 years and Augustus who ruled the Roman Empire for a mere 41. Nowadays few politicians can stand the pace as leaders of governments for more than half a dozen years. So how did Louis XIV survive? He was certainly tough physically - not even the court doctors could kill him. Furthermore he was also strong psychologically; like President Roosevelt of the USA he had a second-class mind but a first-class temperament. Louis combined with these strengths a real taste for administration. In his memoirs he described his job as 'a delightful pastime'. He would have agreed with Noel Coward that 'work is more fun than fun'. But above all Louis was convinced of the validity of what he was trying to do. He had been chosen by God to rule France. 'God has given you all the necessary qualities; all you need do is use them', Mazarin had told the young king. Louis agreed as he confidently embarked on his God-given task.

Louis XIV's professionalism was impressive in a number of ways. He was always well informed, both as a result of personal interviews with specialists and hours of study. In this context Colbert, with his obsession for correct, up-to-date information, was Louis' ideal assistant. The Sun King operated to a methodical pattern of business so that his ministers always knew where to find him and when to have their reports ready; as Saint-Simon observed, with an almanac and a watch one could say a hundred leagues away what the king would be doing. *Le roi bureaucrate* never allowed his pleasures - certainly not his sexual dalliances - to interfere with business. His gluttony did not impair his mental powers and for drunkenness he had contempt. When an ambassador arrived who had a taste for the grape, Louis remarked dryly 'he had better not expect good wine at my table'.

How are we to judge Louis XIV's decision making? No doubt he deceived himself when he reckoned that he took decisions on his own. Like the rest of us, he was influenced by those around him, perhaps more than he realised. Furthermore the crucial question with regard to any leader is, who feeds what information to him. Louvois for instance shielded Louis from the truth about the persecution of the Huguenots. The king was much influenced by Colbert in his early years of power and by Madame de Mainenon towards the end of his life. Even so Louis XIV was never a cypher. He was proud of his qualifications and determined to fulfil his role. His opinions counted for more than those of his advisers; he was the boss. Similarly to depict Louis as wholly dependent on the efficiency of his ministers is wrong. Like any other leader, he needed able assistants. But he chose and led them.

When decisions had to be made, Louis XIV was notoriously slow to make up his mind; 'I will see' was a favourite remark of his. Caution is often a good trait in a ruler, but sometimes Louis allowed it to become indecisiveness. To hurry him up his advisers tended to give the advice which they thought he wanted to hear; the events leading up to the Dutch War (see page 101) illustrate this tendency. To an increasing extent he was surrounded by second-rate advisers whose faces were reassuringly familiar but who were incapable of helping the king to give a firm lead or make up his mind promptly. This may explain some of the disastrous decisions or indecisions in the latter part of his reign.

Furthermore, in old age the Sun King became crotchety and difficult. Saint-Simon reckoned that Louis would accept his ministers' advice on nineteen occasions out of twenty, but would reject it the twentieth time just to show them that he was still the boss. So Torcy, the foreign minister, used to 'nobble' colleagues before a council meeting so that they could present the king with a united front and bring pressure on him to make the right decisions. Perhaps because he suspected that this was going on, Louis took to going behind his ministers' backs, so that Torcy had to try to discover what the king had been saying to his own subordinates. In general the happy trust between king and ministers of the earlier years diminished in the sombre decades of defeat and disaster at the end of the reign.

Our impression of Louis XIV as a team-leader again changes with the years; towards the end of the reign he permitted less discussion and tended to take decisions on his own. However, in the early days of the personal rule Louis welcomed the co-operation of his ministers. It was all rather impressive; indeed the Sun King resembled John F. Kennedy as the hope for the future - that is certainly how contemporaries saw him. The Triad represented experience, the king youthful dynamism; a formidable combination was the result. Louis himself chaired discussions, usually with urbane good humour: 'Colbert will now tell us what the late Cardinal Richelieu would have said'. On other occasions the steel showed through the velvet glove. In 1671, at a meeting of the high council, Colbert protested at a decision of the king's. Two days later the king wrote a letter to his minister.

1 I was master of myself the day before yesterday to conceal from you the sorrow I felt in hearing a man whom I had overwhelmed with benefits talk to me in the fashion you used. I have been very friendly towards you. I still have such a feeling, and I believe I am
5 giving you real proof of it by telling you that I temporarily restrained myself for your sake. I did not wish to tell you what I am writing to you, so as not to give you further opportunity to displease me. It is in the memory of the services that you have done me, and my friendship, which has caused me to do so. Profit
10 thereby and do not risk vexing me again, because after I have heard

your arguments and those of your colleagues, and have given my
opinion on all your claims, I never wish to hear more about it. I am
telling you my honest opinion so that in the future you will be able
to avoid making further false steps.

Once he had made a decision, Louis was not prepared for it to be
questioned, not even by Colbert. On another occasion, when Colbert
had pleaded lack of funds, Louis retorted: 'Have another look at those
figures. If you can't find the money, I'll find someone who can'.
    On the other hand Louis could be a gracious and kind master,
concerned about his servants' welfare. He wrote to Colbert:

1 I have been told that you are not in very good health, and that your
  keenness to return here will be harmful to you. I am writing this
  note to order you to do nothing which will prevent you from
  serving me when you arrive, in all the important tasks which I shall
5 entrust to you. In a word, your health is so vital to me that I wish
  you to conserve it, and to believe that it is my trust in you and my
  friendship which makes me speak in this way.

Louis XIV's man-management is seen at his best in the military context
where he compensated for Louvois' lack of tact in handling aristocratic
and touchy generals. In the summer of 1674 the king told Turenne of his
'entire confidence in your zeal for my service ... I put it in your
judgement to do what you believe to be apropos not doubting that you
will take every possible advantage of the enemy'. After Louvois' death in
1691 Louis took more direct control. 'I am upset to see my army where
it is', he wrote to the dilatory de Lorge. On the other hand Louis
approached the gifted and experienced Marshal Luxembourg with
winning modesty: 'When I give you my thoughts I know that I can teach
you nothing ... I am convinced that if I did not send you my thoughts
you would do as well, or perhaps even better, but *amour propre* makes
one believe that what one says is useful'. To the dejected, defeated
Villeroy after Ramillies (1706) the king said 'at our age, Monsieur, we
can no longer expect to be lucky', a remark as kind as it was fatuous.
Louis retained his flair for man-management to the end. In the crisis of
1709 he chose Villars and Boufflers to command France's armies,
knowing that he could rely on these two old soldiers to co-operate
amicably; they had contempt for France's other generals, with the single
exception of each other.
    Louis XIV deserves the credit for another exercise in man-
management - his domination of the aristocracy. The role of the nobles
in Louis XIV's reign is analysed on page 75. Here we are concerned with
Louis' technique in solving a problem which had much troubled his
predecessors. Louis' secret was the manipulation of faction through the
exploitation of his own personality and the distribution of favours.
Unlike Louis XIII who was only at ease with his favourites or Louis XV

who could be manipulated by an interest-group, Louis XIV remained independent of faction. No group of nobles at court ever monopolised the Sun King's favour, for he remained accessible to all and apparently on good terms with everyone. He had invaluable gifts which enabled him to carry off this act with impressive ease. He was sociable, charming and good-humoured. He had a wonderful memory for faces. He had a great appetite for life, a capacity for enjoying himself and encouraging others to enjoy themselves. For instance he loved showing visitors round his gardens or leading the applause at the theatre - though he himself was the real centre of attention.

Louis XIV also had less attractive qualities which were equally useful when he played factions off against each other. Not only did he have a good memory for faces; he was inquisitive about people's private lives, never forgetting useful information which he had often acquired deviously by opening letters or listening to tittle-tattle. Mazarin advised Louis to 'cultivate that kingly quality of dissimulation which nature has so lavishly bestowed on you'. Behind the impeccable manners lurked a crafty plotter with a malicious delight in setting people on edge, encouraging anxiety and distrust. Louis was utterly cynical, believing that men and women were influenced solely by ambition and greed. The result was that the court of the Sun King became a cockpit in which nobles ruthlessly competed with each other for money and position. 'Who was up? Who was down?' were the questions perpetually on people's lips. Villeroy aptly commented: 'When a minister is in power, you hold his chamber-pot for him, but as soon as you see that his feet are beginning to slide, you empty it over his head'.

So here we see Louis XIV bringing to bear his own particular qualities and style. He showed a shrewd grasp of reality in the way he handled the aristocracy. He was willing to give them a considerable role in running France; by so doing he ensured that there would not be too much resentment at the exclusion of the ancient nobility from the high council and the posts of secretaries of state. At the same time Louis dominated his nobles by his personality, by the exploitation of faction and by reminders that they were dependent on his favour. If nobles wanted wealth and influence, they had to come to court. Louis had them where he wanted them; this was his own personal triumph.

6 What Sort of Absolutism?

Readers will now appreciate that the old picture of Louis XIV as the all-powerful absolutist whose word was unquestioningly obeyed is simplistic. Recent research has demonstrated that it was usually not Louis XIV's way to exploit his theoretically absolute rights by high-profile absolutist actions. His inclination was to compromise, rather than to provoke confrontation. He realised that he was more likely to achieve absolutism by reducing rather than by causing grievances.

Louis XIV's attitude to government was cautious and conservative. Far from trying to overawe the nobles, Louis bribed them with privileges and profits, cynically played them off against each other and at the same time invited them to co-operate with him in the areas of activity where they had traditionally excelled: the army, the Church, diplomacy and local government. The *intendants* were instructed to avoid rather than provoke trouble. The secret of Louis' success as a creator and enforcer of law was co-operation with the *parlements,* and not conflict. The French army was disciplined, and was paid and fed as efficiently as possible so that it would not make a nuisance of itself to civilians. Paris was policed not to subjugate the citizens but to avert disorders. Surprising though it may seem, Louis XIV, supposedly the personification of absolutism, generally ruled by consent.

Perhaps it is the way the French people paid for Louis' wars and other extravagances that best illustrates the nature of his monarchy. Why did they pay? There is an obvious explanation: the people of France were forced to pay. But this is not the whole story, and we cannot explain the very remarkable and indeed puzzling readiness of the tax-payers to pay by simply shouting 'absolutism'. We need to establish who forced whom to pay, how and why. The truth is that the whole tax-paying process in Louis XIV's France was a gigantic racket in which the king and his more favoured subjects connived at each others' greed at the expense of the poor. The people who benefited from this unholy alliance were the governing classes, the financiers, the office-holders, the tax-farmers, the richer peasants. And this was not simply because they did not pay the taxes. It was because they made huge profits out of taxing the unfortunates who did pay. On occasions taxes were indeed extracted by force, by the use of troops. But for most of the time the non-paying exploited the helplessness and the vulnerability of the unprivileged who were badgered, blackmailed and bullied into paying.

Equally instructive is the story of armed revolt in Louis XIV's reign. Although it was a violent age, there was remarkably little organised rebellion - a significant contrast with previous reigns. Was this because an absolute king was able to deter potential rebels through fear of the consequences? Louis was quite prepared to use force against his own subjects as his instructions to Turenne made clear:

1 We find ourselves obliged for the conservation of the state as much as for its glory and reputation, to maintain in peace as well as in war a great number of troops, both infantry and cavalry, which will always be in good condition to act to keep our people in the
5 obedience and respect they owe, to insure the peace and tranquillity that we have won.

Troops were used against revolts around Boulogne in 1662, in Brittany in 1675 and against the Camisards of the Cevennes between 1702 and 1705.

However, this impression of absolutist triumph over rebellion needs to be qualified. Revolts were few and ineffectual because the government was careful not to provoke the powerful and the influential; compromise was the order of the day. So it remained even against rebels. The Bretons were dealt with mercifully; only 24 leaders were executed, the royal governor agreed to summon the Estates in order to hear grievances, and royal troops were ordered not to victimise the populace. Even more significant was the Camisard revolt for here the government forces failed to achieve a victory; the rebels' demand - to be allowed to practise their Protestant religion - was conceded; the king's representative, a Marshal of France, negotiated with a baker's son. Again, this a far cry from the absolutism of the text-books.

There is therefore a strong case for questioning the traditional, oversimplified picture of Louis XIV as an absolute king. His government was faced with the complexities and inbuilt privileges of French society plus the widespread determination to obstruct and ignore royal edicts. Even by the end of the reign no single law applied through the whole of France; for instance the revocation of the Edict of Nantes did not affect Alsace. The fact that Colbert had to repeat instructions over and over again tells its own story. In 1665 the great minister attempted to abolish the *paulette*. Predictably this produced a storm of protest from influential office-holders, and so the king told Colbert to abandon the idea. In the real world in which they lived, Louis XIV and his ministers had to manoeuvre, make concessions and temper absolutism with opportunism.

Indeed there is a case for saying that Louis XIV's rule was in theory absolute but not arbitrary, while in practice it was the opposite. Occasionally when defied or provoked, he lashed out vindictively - the classic behaviour of the arbitrary tyrant. Mousnier considers the persecution of the Huguenots to have been Louis' chief tyrannical act. One could quote the devastation of the Palatinate as another instance (see page 116), or the victimisation of Fouquet. Were these Louis' vindictive reactions to his own frustration and impotence? Possibly.

However, on no account should we forget that Louis XIV enormously increased the power of the Crown. He ruthlessly achieved an ordered, disciplined and obedient people. He recruited the armed forces, the Church, the law and the media in his campaign to establish royal authority and to eradicate dissidents; hence his persecution of Protestants and Jansenists (see pages 36 and 43). He operated a successful machine for extracting the maximum amount of money from the tax-payers. He developed a vast bureaucracy, venal, hereditary and cumbersome, but he also built up a royal bureaucracy ultimately dependent on his favour. Louis' combination of control over the army and domination of the aristocracy delivered the Crown from the nightmare of armed rebellion by overmighty subjects. He achieved a monopoly of the means of coercion. He was far more successful than either his predecessors or his successors.

There was in fact an essential brittleness about Louis XIV's absolutism, in that to an enormous extent it depended on his own exceptional skills. For his success was due to his street-wise realism, his hard-nosed awareness of the advantages to be derived by manipulating patronage and privilege. Over the conflicting rivalries of noblemen, financiers and administrators he remained the arbiter. This fragility was concealed by a skilfully orchestrated media-offensive (see page 82). It is partly due to the success of this public-relations campaign that Louis' absolutism has been exaggerated both by contemporaries and historians. While his armies were defeated and he was obliged to bargain and conciliate at home, his propaganda conquered Europe. Thus was created the myth of absolutism.

Our task is to pin-point the reality. Here we have to make a choice. On the one hand with hindsight we know that Louis XIV's absolutism was far more limited than his more traditional critics have appreciated. On the other hand, the reader must decide how far revisionism should go. When all due qualifications have been made, there is a case for concluding that, given the context in which he operated, Louis XIV was remarkably successful. Did he not indeed make absolutism work?

Making notes on *The Politics of Absolutism*

Bearing in mind the current controversy between historians about whether Louis XIV was or was not an absolutist king, you need to understand what absolutism was and what the alleged advantages were of adopting an absolutist approach. So you should begin with a note on the definition of absolutism followed by a summary of what contemporaries understood by the term. Then analyse Louis XIV's inheritance: the background to the personal rule with especial emphasis on the problems which apparently justified Louis' resort to absolutist methods, plus the machinery of government which he took over from Cardinal Mazarin.

You then need to detail the development of the system. To what extent was Louis an innovator? Take the point hinted at in the text that some historians consider that Louis did not change very much in his manipulation of the levers of power. In which case what *was* distinctive about Louis XIV's system of government? Note separately his development of royal power with respect to the law, the armed forces and local government. Make explicit notes on how Louis got hold of the money which he needed for his foreign policy and his domestic expenses. Similarly be sure to analyse in note form how he dominated the aristocracy. Indicate that you should also refer to your notes on chapter 5. Make a special note on Louis XIV's qualities and defects as a team-leader and a decision-maker. Likewise, list Louis' debts to his ministers: how vital was their contribution?

So was Louis XIV an absolute ruler? Examiners are liable to raise this question. Note the strong case for arguing that Louis was indeed absolute: the significant increase in royal power, the remarkable achievements of the reign, and the almost total disappearance of organised opposition. On the other hand, be able to enlarge on the case for questioning whether he really was an absolute monarch. Note the compromises which he had to make, and the limitations on his power.

Answering essay questions on *The Politics of Absolutism*

This is an area in which recent research has questioned the assumptions of the textbooks. As you will have discovered from reading this chapter, Louis XIV's power was limited, he compromised and manoeuvred and there is a real case for saying that 'absolutism' does not describe the reality of government in seventeenth-century France. On the other hand, you may want to argue that revisionism has gone too far. In these circumstances there is much to be said for sending out a signal to the examiner that you are aware of 'recent research'. Or, better still, name such historians as Roger Mettam or David Parker if you have been able to consult their works (see the Further Reading section on page 151).

Examiners often raise the following issues. How did the system work? How did Louis XIV get his results? Did all this amount to absolutism?

1 Examine the strengths and weaknesses of Louis XIV as ruler of France.
2 How tyrannical was Louis XIV?
3 'Louis XIV's greatest political skill was to choose capable ministers'. Do you agree?
4 To what extent was Louis XIV an innovator as ruler of France?
5 To what extent can Louis XIV's kingship be described as 'absolutism'?
6 How far did Louis XIV overcome the handicaps and obstacles to absolute government in France?

Common to all these questions is the implicit assumption that Louis XIV inherited a difficult situation. This a good point to consider in the introduction. Given the apparent handicaps under which he operated, how do we explain Louis' relative success?

Let us take the question 'How is Louis XIV's success as ruler of France to be explained?' In your introduction you must define Louis' success, that is to say, explain what for the purposes of this essay you mean by 'success'. During your development section - the main part of your essay, between your introduction and your conclusion - you should consider possible explanations: that he chose efficient ministers, that his methods were tyrannical, that somehow he discovered a new approach to government, that he was absolute, that he was prepared to manoeuvre and compromise, that he used patronage effectively. Two particular warnings will, I hope, be helpful. First, be careful to define such words as 'tyranny' and 'absolutism'. Secondly, be as precise as possible, avoiding vague and wishy-washy expressions such as 'Louis won the respect of the nobility', or 'Louis had public opinion on his side' or again, and most dangerous, 'Louis succeeded because he was an absolute king'. You must explain how and why he won the nobles' respect, what evidence there is that public opinion was on his side, and what you mean by 'absolute'. In your conclusion stress explanations which you consider to be convincing.

Making an overall judgement of Louis XIV's professional expertise is difficult. It is essential to give a clear answer to the question. But do not be afraid of admitting that the whole truth is elusive or that historians disagree. This is particularly the case if the concept of absolutism is involved. Methodical study of the first and last sections of this chapter should help you. Also consult the Conclusion, where Louis XIV's overall competence is assessed.

Source-based questions on *The Politics of Absolutism*

1 The Personal Rule in Action

Carefully study Louis XIV's announcement of his intention to rule personally (page 12) and his letters to Colbert and Turenne (pages 25, 26 and 28). Answer the following questions.

a) What can be concluded from Louis' announcement about his motives for ruling personally? (4 marks)

b) What sort of a man-manager emerges from Louis' communications to his subordinates? (4 marks)

c) What problems lay behind Louis' letter to Turenne? (2 marks)

d) Do these documents suggest that Louis XIV's ambition to rule personally was achieved? Explain your answer by detailed reference to the extracts. (5 marks)

2 Louis XIV's Ministers Contrasted

Carefully read Colbert's letters to his *intendants* and assistants and the description of Louvois rebuking the courtier, (pages 19, 21 and 22). Answer the following questions.

a) What evidence do the extracts contain to suggest that Colbert and Louvois were very different as man-managers? (4 marks)

b) Would it be right to conclude from these sources that courtiers were more idle and less professional than *intendants?* Explain your answer. (3 marks)

c) Does the evidence here suggest that Colbert served his king more effectively than Louvois? Explain your answer. (3 marks)

d) Which source do you think gives the best picture of the real state of affairs in Louis XIV's reign? Explain your answer. (5 marks)

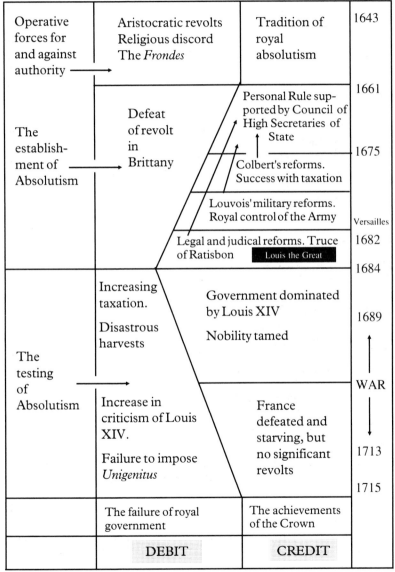

Operative forces for and against authority →	Aristocratic revolts Religious discord The *Frondes*	Tradition of royal absolutism	1643
The establishment of Absolutism →	Defeat of revolt in Brittany →	Personal Rule supported by Council of High Secretaries of State ↑ Colbert's reforms. Success with taxation Louvois' military reforms. Royal control of the Army Legal and judical reforms. Truce of Ratisbon Louis the Great	1661 1675 Versailles 1682 1684
The testing of Absolutism →	Increasing taxation. Disastrous harvests	Government dominated by Louis XIV Nobility tamed	1689 ↑ WAR ↓
	Increase in criticism of Louis XIV. Failure to impose *Unigenitus*	France defeated and starving, but no significant revolts	1713 1715
	The failure of royal government	The achievements of the Crown	
	DEBIT	CREDIT	

Summary: The Politics of Absolutism

CHAPTER 3

Louis XIV and Religion

1 The Background

Louis XIV's approach to religion was straightforward. He was a devout Catholic in the tradition of the Counter-Reformation, the movement which had reformed the Catholic Church. Throughout his life he attended mass daily and with his chin resting on the top of his cane listened intently to his court preachers. But he was no theologian and inherited from his mother an impatience with doctrinal niceties.

Louis however was encouraged to take his religious duties seriously by his confessors who were invariably members of the Society of Jesus (or Jesuits, as they were commonly known). These 'shock troops of the Counter-Reformation' were noted for their dedication and their devotion to Rome. Louis was a willing pupil. He earnestly tried to 'further the interests of heaven', the Jesuit phrase for promoting the Catholic Church. And at the same time he did his best to save his own soul and those of his subjects, for Louis never forgot that he was a king and not a private person, and that the spiritual welfare of eighteen and a half million souls had been entrusted to him.

Religion profoundly coloured contemporary conceptions of monarchy. It was generally accepted that kings inherited their thrones by divine right - that is to say, they did not rule by the consent of their subjects but were chosen by God. Most people thought that to resist an anointed king was blasphemy. Louis believed this and applied it to himself. He liked to be compared to his saintly ancestor, Louis IX, and throughout his reign he laid his hands on sufferers from scrofula, known as the king's evil, because it could only be cured by the touch of an anointed king. No wonder that Louis could claim: 'Holding as it were the place of God we seem to participate in His knowledge'.

Louis was proud of the tradition whereby the King of France was called the 'Eldest Son of the Church' and the 'Most Christian King'. He also valued the title which was given him at his birth - *le dieudonné* (the gift of God). Born to middle-aged, seemingly incompatible parents, Louis was the miracle child, sent to save France from spiritual disunity and chaos. He believed in order and authority and did not hesitate to intervene personally and decisively in religious affairs.

2 Louis XIV's Relations with the Papacy

It was in the mutual interests of both Papacy and French Crown that their relationship should be cordial. Pope and king could give each other support against disruptive elements in the Church and state. This desirable state of affairs had prevailed since the early sixteenth century. It might seem surprising therefore that for much of his reign Louis XIV and his papal contemporaries were on bad terms.

Part of the explanation is that so much was at stake. As we have seen Louis XIV had a high opinion of his kingly office. He therefore felt justified in supervising the spiritual welfare of the French Church despite the Pope's claims to be the supreme authority. As the Most Christian King and as the successor of St Louis, the Sun King reformed the Church and even interfered in doctrinal matters. Furthermore there was the question of money. Who was to exploit the immense financial assets of the Church, the income from benefices, the right to appoint to rich livings? Nor should we forget the influence of the clergy in social and political matters. Whoever controlled the pulpit more or less controlled public opinion throughout France.

The struggle for the domination of the French Church had always been a three-cornered affair between the Papacy, the Crown and the nobles. Since the fourteenth century the movement known as Gallicanism had campaigned for the freedom of the French Church from papal influence, both in spiritual and temporal affairs. To a great extent this had been an aristocratic movement, deriving its strength from the ambitions of the French nobility, anxious to dominate the Church as much as the state. Gallicanism was a potential threat to the Crown as well as to the Papacy. Hence the alliance between Louis XIV's predecessors and Rome - although Gallicanism had never been totally suppressed. It could of course become the king's ally against Rome if that was the way the king wished to play his hand.

In 1661 the young king was full of self-confidence and had no intention of kowtowing to anyone, not even the Pope. So when there was a fracas in August 1662 between the Pope's Corsican guards and the French ambassador's guards in Rome, the king demanded and received a full apology; the Pope even consented to the construction of a monument recording his humiliation. This however was a bagatelle, and in February 1665 the Pope obligingly issued a bull (an official papal pronouncement) condemning the Jansenists against whom Louis was waging a vendetta (see page 43). For his part, Louis XIV was glad to accept the Pope's lead in patching up a compromise with Jansenism in 1669.

However, real problems were caused by a royal declaration in 1673 that the king was entitled to the *régale* in all parts of the realm. This was an ancient custom by which the king appropriated the revenues of vacant bishoprics; it had formerly operated in northern France only. Two bishops in the Midi appealed against their king to Rome. Pope Innocent XI appreciated that it was not simply a question of money but of the king's claim unilaterally to alter the customs of the Church. He therefore supported the bishops by threatening to censure the Eldest Son of the Church unless he backed down.

Louis XIV's response was to let loose the Gallicans. You did not have to scratch French ecclesiastics very hard in order to reveal hatred of

Roman influence. Bishops influenced by Gallicanism led the way at an assembly of the French clergy 'gathered in Paris by royal command'. In March 1682 they published the so-called Gallican Articles. These were anti-papal, pronouncing that 'kings and princes were not subordinate to Rome in non-spiritual matters', that 'in spiritual matters popes were inferior to general councils' and that 'the pope's decisions could be altered if they did not have the approval of the whole church'. These sentiments were highly offensive to Rome.

Things soon went from bad to worse. Innocent XI refused to consecrate any more French bishops so that before long no less than 35 dioceses were unfilled. In January 1687 he cancelled the immunity of the French embassy in Rome from inspection by officials pursuing criminals. When Louis told his ambassador to defy the papal authorities, the Pope excommunicated the ambassador and prepared to excommunicate Louis XIV as well. The nadir was reached over the issue of the Cologne election. This episode is dealt with on page 113. Suffice it here to record that Louis XIV's defiance of the Pope now blew up in his face, wrecking his foreign policy. Louis' retaliatory gesture of seizing the papal state of Avignon in southern France embarrassed French Catholics and appalled public opinion throughout Europe. The Most Christian King put himself completely in the wrong by this blatant aggression.

In fact Louis XIV now realised that he had gone too far. Rather late in the day he appreciated that there was more to be gained than lost by co-operation with Rome. Reconciliation was assisted by the death of Innocent XI in 1689. In 1693 Louis withdrew the Gallican Articles and a compromise was achieved over the *régale*. Louis XIV was especially anxious to mend his fences with Rome because he again needed papal support against the French Jansenists (see page 43).The Sun King's relations with the Papacy therefore has this bizarre conclusion: he had to appeal to the Pope in order to impose his policies on his own people.

3 The Huguenots

French Protestantism dated from the mid-sixteenth century. Its theology was Calvinist and it was from Calvin's Geneva that the movement derived its organisation and its inspiration. These French Calvinists were known as Huguenots. Initially their leadership was aristocratic. The last Valois kings - Charles IX (1560-74) and Henri III (1574-89) - faced armed rebellion from their Huguenot nobles who virtually controlled a state within a state. In 1589 their leader, the Bourbon prince Henri of Navarre, inherited the throne as Henri IV. To win the support of the majority of Frenchmen, Henri became a Catholic. After his conversion, however, he was forced to make concessions to the Huguenots in order to bring peace to an exhausted nation; by the Edict of Nantes (1598) not only were the Huguenots given freedom of worship but they also received substantial military and political guarantees.

In retrospect the Edict of Nantes seems a milestone in history. For the first time two religions were tolerated in one state, surely a victory for Henri of Navarre's common sense and decency. But this is not how it appeared to contemporaries who believed that religious disunity meant political disunity. Catholic Frenchmen were ashamed of the Edict of Nantes, regarding it as a regrettable necessity; it had been sealed with yellow rather than with the green wax of permanent royal edicts. In 1629 Richelieu negotiated the Grace of Alais which abolished the political and military clauses of the Edict of Nantes. Although the religious clauses were confirmed, most Frenchmen thought that the sooner they too were abolished, the better.

This was certainly Louis XIV's opinion. He did not like Protestants. He had been brought up to detest heresy and at his coronation he had promised to extirpate it. He regarded the very existence of the Huguenot churches as a challenge and an insult to the Most Christian King. His confessors assured him that heretics were damned and that it was therefore a kindness to convert them by all possible means. So it was that in 1659 a delegation of Huguenots from Toulouse received a frosty reception from the Sun King. It soon became apparent that both the letter and the spirit of the law had a new interpreter.

Between 1661 and 1679 Huguenots were not physically persecuted but they were made to feel uncomfortable. Restrictions were imposed on their marriages and funerals. Schools and churches were closed. Huguenots were bribed to abandon their faith, the revenues of vacant bishoprics being devoted to this objective. A special government department, the *casse des conversions*, handled this business; its leader, Paul Pellisson, claimed to have converted fifty thousand at the rate of ten *livres* a head. In 1668 one of the king's best generals, the Huguenot Turenne, became a Catholic - a blow to Huguenot morale. It is difficult to arrive at reliable statistics, but during these years the total number of Huguenots may have fallen from two million to one and a quarter million. If these policies had been continued, the Huguenot community might have disappeared completely by about 1750.

However, we shall never know, for in 1679 Louis XIV opted for a more aggressive policy. His objectives remained the same - the eradication of heresy and a unified Church and state. But his tactics changed. The king and his more enthusiastic clergy (known as the *dévots*) believed that they had the Huguenots on the run. The mild policies adopted hitherto might snuff out Protestantism in the next century, but Louis and his advisers thought that 'the interests of heaven' could be more speedily served. They believed that with decisive strokes the game would be won.

Why Louis abandoned tactics which from his point of view were working well has been much discussed. Certainly the peace of Nymegen (February 1679) allowed him to concentrate on domestic affairs and the total elimination of heresy. Nor did Louis need flatterers to tell him that he was at the height of his powers: how ridiculous therefore that the Most Christian King, the hammer of the heretical Dutch, should be defied by heretics at home! The Huguenots might no longer be a state within the state, but by their very existence they spoilt national unity; it was high time to put things right. Furthermore, the king was under pressure from the *dévot* party to save his own soul and the souls of his heretical subjects. Court gossip made much of Madame de Maintenon's role. She had convinced the king that his sexual promiscuity had been unpleasing to God, and that he could only put matters right by converting heretics. Certainly the ruthlessness with which de Maintenon enforced the conversion of her own relatives suggested that she believed that the end justified the means.

Whatever Louis' motives may have been, a more abrasive campaign was now launched. First, the *Chambres de l'Edit* - courts which had protected the interests of Huguenots - were abolished. Then in June 1680 all conversions from Catholicism to Protestantism were forbidden. Huguenot churches were demolished on the flimsiest of pretexts, such as the celebration of mixed marriages, and often without any pretext at all. Huguenots were banned from public office and from the medical, legal and publishing professions. Their children were taken from them at the age of seven to be educated as Catholics.

At the same time Huguenots were assailed by offensive and tendentious propaganda. The pastoral proclamation of July 1682 is a good example:

1 Long has the church of Christ poured forth her supplications for you, most dear brethren, and has beheld you with sincere concern and affliction separated from her and lost in the frightful solitude of error, ever since by a voluntary schism you have cut yourself off
5 from her. What remains to be done by you, but only to forget this schism in which you are fallen and rather to choose to return to your Father's house where even the hired servants live in plenty and abundance: while you who are his children find nothing but husks to support you in your weakness, in your spiritual thirst and
10 hunger which so dreadfully consumes you. Why then do you deliberate and whence is it that you hold out and oppose us? Is it because you think it a shame to resume the name and quality of children of the church, while Louis the Great, her eldest son, makes it the height of his glory to raise every day new trophies in
15 honour of so worthy a mother? Is his happinesss then bounded by your obstinacy only? The only disappointment which remains to him is to see still a number of his subjects so many enemies of his religion and deserters of the ancient christian warfare. But if you refuse to do this and because this last error would be more criminal
20 in you than all others, you ought to expect from it misfortunes

incomparably more terrible than all those which your revolt and
your schism have at present pulled down upon you. We expect
from you, most dear brethren, better sentiments and designs more
favourable to your salvation.

Huguenots soon discovered the meaning of 'misfortunes incomparably
more terrible'. The billeting of troops had always been unpopular.
Marillac, the *intendant* in Poitou, now quartered dragoons on
recalcitrant Protestants. Far from attempting to control these troops, the
authorities encouraged them to misbehave. Men were beaten up,
women raped, children terrorised, and property ruined. Thomas
Bureau, a Huguenot bookseller at Niort in Poitou, described the
conduct of dragoons quartered on his family in August 1685:

1 Four were sent to our house where they began with the shop. They
   threw all the books onto the ground, brought their horses into the
   shop and used the books as litter. Then they went through the
   rooms where they threw everything into the street. I had written to
5 my mother to persuade her to conceal herself with my sister. But
   that was virtually impossible, for catholics are forbidden to offer
   refuge to protestants on pain of the galleys. The commander of the
   dragoons shouted at my mother: 'You bitch, you still have not
   changed your religion, and neither has your whore of a daughter.
10 You bugger of a bitch, you really are for it now'.

When the king heard about this unorthodox evangelism, he was
annoyed, for he was not a cruel man. Louvois redeployed Marillac and
explained to his *intendants* that 'violence is not to the taste of His
Majesty'. But the 'dragonnades' continued. So did financial pressure.
Converts to Catholicism were exempted from *taille* - the tax which
virtually everyone had to pay - while heretics had their assessment
quadrupled.

Not surprisingly these tactics proved effective. Bishops and *intendants*
vied with one another in producing conversion statistics. In fact, the
ecclesiastical authorities had difficulty providing instruction for new
converts. In the meantime further harassment was introduced.
Members of the public who denounced Huguenots were rewarded with
half their property. Protestants were forbidden to preach or to write.
They were not allowed to employ Catholic servants. They were not
allowed to emigrate, although ministers who broke the law forbidding
them to preach were banished or sent to the galleys.

Against this background the revocation of the Edict of Nantes might
seem merely the official seal of approval. Indeed, one of its justifications
was that the 'so-called reformed religion' had ceased to exist. In this
respect Louis may well have believed his own propaganda. However, his
chief motive was to challenge the Emperor Leopold's claim to be the

foremost Catholic monarch. Leopold had just defeated the heathen Turks - to the mortification of the Most Christian King, who really should have been at the Emperor's side. So Louis was determined to counter imperial self-congratulations by striking a significant blow against heresy at home.

The revocation was promulgated by the Edict of Fontainebleau, registered by the *parlement* of Paris on 22 October 1685. The preamble explained how 'Henri the Great, our grandfather of glorious memory' granted privileges to members of the so-called reformed religion in order that France could have peace and christian unity could be re-established. Unfortunately Henri the Great was murdered before his dearest wishes could be achieved. Due to the Huguenots' disruptive behaviour 'the late king our father' removed several of their privileges. It had always been the intention of Louis' grand-father, his father and himself 'to unite to the church those who had so easily strayed from it'. Success had clearly been achieved 'since the better and greater part of our subjects of the said so-called reformed religion have embraced Catholicism; and since for that reason the execution of the Edict of Nantes remains pointless we have come to the conclusion that in order to wipe out all memory of the troubles, confusion and evil caused in our kingdom by the progress of that false religion, we cannot do better than revoke the said Edict entirely'. Then followed clauses totally banning public Protestant worship, banishing ministers who refused to conform, insisting that children of Protestants should be baptised and educated in the Catholic religion and condemning to the galleys laymen who tried to emigrate.

The immediate results of the revocation were tragic for all concerned. Not even Louis XIV could close his frontiers to the thousands who were desperate to escape. Despite 1,450 would-be fugitives being sent to the galleys, approximately 200,000 Huguenots emigrated to Holland, Brandenburg, England and the New World, taking with them their skills, their memories of France and their hatred of Louis XIV. Ten thousand Huguenots fought for William of Orange in the coming wars, including Marshal Schomberg and 600 other officers. Huguenots who remained were subjected to forced conversions, forced attendance at mass, and forced protestations of loyalty. Persecution escalated. Between 1685 and 1762 46 Huguenot ministers were executed and 16 who had fled from France were hanged in effigy. Not even the dead were spared. The corpses of relapsed heretics were dragged naked through the streets, left on rubbish dumps to be devoured by rats and arranged in obscene positions to the scandal of their bereaved relations.

In the longer term the campaign against the Huguenots failed in its main purpose. In remote areas, such as the Midi, Protestant congregations continued to worship, while Huguenots revolted in the Cevannes in 1689 and in 1692. In July 1702 the murder of a prominent persecutor, the abbé du Chayla, led to the Camisards war. At a time when France was fighting for her life, Louis had to dispatch troops, dismiss a general whose brutality had proved counter-productive and permit Villars, a marshal of France, to concede toleration to the Camisard rebels. So much had persecution achieved. Protestant worship continued throughout the eighteenth century until it was officially legalised by Napoleon.

Can one disagree with the claim of Roland Mousnier, a modern French historian, that Louis XIV's treatment of Protestants was not only pointless and ineffectual but tyrannical? 'The methods he used were inhuman, an affront to the dignity of man and contrary to the spirit of Christianity while forced communion was a sin against the Holy Ghost'. Perhaps Mousnier exceeded the historian's brief by making a moral judgement. However, Louis' reputation has certainly been harmed by his persecution of the Huguenots. Even the Pope observed that Christ had not used soldiers in order to convert people.

Whether or not Louis' treatment of the Huguenots was a crime, most historians regard the revocation as a blunder. The emigration of so many merchants, bankers and craftsmen was France's loss and Europe's gain. Although research has proved that Louis' wars harmed the economy more than the revocation, nevertheless Huguenots certainly taught France's rivals how to produce high quality goods such as gloves, headware, silk, glass and varnish. Cardinals' hats were now made in England.

In the context of international relations, Louis XIV's campaign against the Huguenots unquestionably damaged his own cause. Immediate results disappointed the king. If Louis hoped that by hounding Protestants he would capture the leadership of Catholic Europe, he was speedily disabused; Catholics continued to take their lead from an anti-French Pope and a conquering Emperor. As for longer-term effects, these were highly damaging to Louis' interests, for the obvious beneficiary from the campaign against the Huguenots was William of Orange, soon to become William III of England.

It is easy to forget how many obstacles William encountered when he built up his anti-French alliance. James II's England was a French satellite. The Dutch Estates had distrusted the Orange dynasty for decades and wished to remain at peace with France. Nevertheless, William invaded and recruited England, defying European public opinion by chasing out James II, his own father-in-law. He persuaded both the English and the Dutch political nations to follow him into two costly European wars. The Emperor Leopold disapproved of alliances with heretics; yet he joined heretics in fighting the Most Christian King.

William was assisted by Louis' campaign against the Huguenots. In order to convince the English parliament, the Dutch estates and the emperor that in their own interests they should join him, William represented the King of France as a menace. William's propagandists - many of them Huguenots - could now depict Louis as a persecutor, keen to put the clock back to an unhappier age. The peace and stability of Europe would be disrupted by unlimited *dragonnades* if Louis was allowed to have his way. It was essential to stop his campaign to establish a universal monarchy based on a universal religion.

On the other hand, Louis XIV's persecution of the Huguenots was certainly popular among Catholic Frenchmen. The clergy were especially enthusiastic. They assured the king that by bringing pressure to bear on the Huguenots he was putting into practice 'compel them to come in' (the parable of the great supper). Bossuet, Bishop of Meaux, exemplified this approval in his defence of the revocation:

> 1 Let us not fail to proclaim this miracle of our age and to perpetuate its record. You who inscribe the annals of the church take up the pen of a ready writer and hasten to give Louis his place with Constantine and Theodosius. Let us raise our acclamations even
> 5 to the skies, attributing to this new Theodosius, this new Marcion, this new Charlemagne the words of the six hundred and thirty fathers of the council of Chalcedon: 'You have confirmed the faith; you have exterminated heretics.' This is the crowning achievement of your reign which thereby gains a character all of its own.
> 10 Because of you heresy is no more.

The revocation did indeed give Louis' reign a character all of its own. Bossuet's somewhat obsequious comments reflected a real consensus among Louis' Catholic subjects. In the immediate aftermath of the revocation the king was rapturously received in Paris. 'Never had so much adulation been manifested. The acclamations were never-ending. A hundred thousand voices cried out "long live the king!"'. The fact is that the Huguenots were generally unpopular. Many were envied for their wealth. Many were just as bigoted as French Catholics - or for that matter English Protestants. Many refused to show respect for public manifestations of Catholic piety. Clearly there were limits to Louis' absolutism and to a very real extent therefore his policies had to command popular support. The revocation of the Edict of Nantes illustrates this truth. Indeed, Louis' biographer Bluche has gone as far as to claim that given public opinion Louis had no option but to revoke.

If Bluche overstates this argument, he plausibly maintains that the revocation brought solid advantages. He questions whether Louis' most impressive diplomatic *coup* - the accession of his grandson Philip to the throne of Spain in 1701 - would have been possible without the revocation; would the Spaniards have accepted Philip as their king if he had been the grandson of a ruler who tolerated heretics? Bluche argues that Louis' new subjects in Flanders and Franche-Comté were impressed by the achievement of religious unity. And only the revocation could have inspired the self-sacrifice of the French people when the old king appealed for unity in the crisis of 1709-11.

However, not only France's enemies believed that the persecution of the Huguenots was regrettable. Louis' sister-in-law, Liselotte wrote:

1 The old trollop and Father La Chaize persuaded the king that all
  the sins he had committed with the Montespan would be forgiven
  if he persecuted the Huguenots and by so doing he would get to
  heaven. The poor king believed every word, for never in his life had
5 he read one word of the Bible. This was the origin of the vicious
  persecution which we had seen.

Vauban deplored the revocation, comparing it with the expulsion of the useful and blameless Mohammedan Moriscoes by Philip III of Spain at the beginning of the century. Their 'crimes' were their religion and their race. For that matter parallels with Hitler's persecution of the Jews are valid - although there are obvious contrasts as well.

Perhaps the most revealing comparison is an ironic one. In the 1870s Bismarck tried to destroy Catholicism in Germany, believing that Catholics were 'enemies of the Reich'. His contention was that it was impossible to be both a good Catholic and a good German. Like Bismarck, Louis had a craving for unity and order. The Huguenots were different and therefore a blemish. So they must be erased even though such a course was contrary to sense and human decency. And the comparison with Bismarck can be taken further still. Whereas Philip III and Hitler were only too successful as racist persecutors, both Louis XIV and Bismarck failed. For creeds thrive on persecution.

4 Jansenism

The story of Louis XIV's dealings with Jansenism is complex. This is partly because there was disagreement about the nature and extent of Jansenism. Furthermore, Jansenism proved to be the catalyst for disputes over wider issues. Louis XIV's exalted conception of monarchy encouraged him to adopt a high-handed, authoritarian attitude towards Jansenism. The resulting conflicts raised questions about the French Church's freedom from both papal and royal interference.

Jansenism can be traced back to the publication of Cornelius Jansen's book *Augustinus* in 1640, two years after his death. Jansen attributed to St. Paul and St. Augustine the doctrine that man was hopelessly sinful and could only be saved by the grace of God. This appeared to conflict with the Jesuits' emphasis on people's freedom of choice and of the value in God's sight of their good deeds. Sound Christian arguments were advanced by both Jesuits and Jansenists, who protested their loyalty to the Catholic Church. The fact that Jansenists were people of blameless lives and great learning indicated that 'they were simply good Catholics who were disapproved of by the Jesuits'. This disapproval did the

Jansenists no harm in France, because the Jesuits were disliked for their subservience to Rome and for their apparent willingness to justify virtually anything if it suited them. By contrast the Jansenists impressed by their intellectual honesty and by the high moral standards at the monastery of Port-Royal des Champs, their unofficial headquarters just outside Paris. Port-Royal compared favourably with the alleged laxity of the French Church as a whole.

Louis XIV could make little of Jansenism; all he knew was that he did not like it. His Jesuit confessors advised him that the Jansenists were a disruptive influence. Louis was aware that opponents of royal government during his adolescence such as the duchesse de Longueville were tarred with Jansenism. He was convinced that the Jansenists were a threat to the stability of the French Church and kingdom. Louis was in no way mollified by Jansenist claims that they were misrepresented. Certainly confusion spread because 'Jansenist' became a general term of abuse rather like 'fascist' in our own times. Once Louis rejected someone for a post who had been described as a Jansenist. When the applicant turned out to be an atheist, the king gave him the job. He knew where he stood with an atheist whereas Jansenists were awkward people who defied the king's authority by thinking for themselves. Perhaps 'bolshies' would be a suitable modern equivalent.

It is surprising that Louis was unimpressed by the high moral standards of the Jansenists because he was aware of the defects of the French Church as a whole. To his credit he defended the playwright Molière against the queen and the *dévots* when they demanded the suppression of *Tartuffe,* an attack on contemporary religious hypocrisy. The *dévots* were offended by passages such as the following, in which Tartuffe attempts to steal his friend's fortune:

Worldly wealth makes little appeal to me. Its tawdry glitter doesn't dazzle me. If I resolve to accept this fortune it's only because I fear that such possessions may fall into unworthy hands or pass to people who will use them for evil purposes and not employ them as I intend to do to the glory of God and the good of my neighbour.

Much though Louis appreciated this satire, he preferred to reform the Catholic Church himself rather than take lessons from the Jansenists. The influence of the Counter-Reformation was certainly alive in France. During Louis XIV's reign there was a steady improvement in the education and training of parish priests. Aristocratic absentee bishops haunting the corridors of Versailles were more typical of the mid-eighteenth century. Louis took trouble over episcopal appointments, promoting men on their merits as well as because of their birth. As a result diocesan seminaries thrived, conferences to update parish priests' theology met regularly and a French bishop who boasted that he was the least ecclesiastical churchman that the world had ever seen became the exception rather than the rule.

So Louis' approach to the Jansenist problem was to take the wind out of their sails by reforming the French Church, while at the same time repressing Jansenist influence. This was logical given his belief in the necessity of uniformity and discipline. In 1661 he imposed Jesuit doctrines on Port-Royal and chased out the male Jansenist leaders. Three years later the nuns were expelled from Port-Royal by the Archbishop of Paris, who - perhaps significantly - had once been Louis XIV's tutor. The hostile, indeed hysterical, attitude of the royal ecclesiastical establishment towards Jansenism can be gauged by the archbishop's abuse of the abbess, a woman of maturity and erudition:

1 Be quiet! You are nothing more than a proud and stubborn little woman, without the sense to see that you meddle in matters which you do not understand . You are nothing more than a stuck-up slip of a girl, a poor fool, an ignoramus who doesn't know what to say.
5 You may be as pure as an angel but you are as proud as Lucifer. Off with you! Be off with you!.

Only after expressions of penitence were the nuns allowed to return.

However, Jansenism continued to be a force even though Louis XIV persecuted Jansenists as and when the opportunities arose. He soon discovered that much depended on the co-operation of Rome, for only the Pope could condemn Jansenism with the necessary finality to counter the respect which Jansenists enjoyed among thoughtful and educated Frenchmen. Louis therefore welcomed an anti-Jansenist bull which Pope Alexander VII issued in February 1665.

Unfortunately several French bishops disagreed with the Pope and the king in their condemnation of Jansenist doctrine. The Jesuits argued that 'Paul begat Augustine, Augustine begat Calvin, Calvin begat Jansen'. But this was really too much for most intelligent, unprejudiced Catholics. Furthermore, as we have seen, French Catholics could easily be influenced by Gallican resentment against papal interference. As a result, between 1668 and 1679 the anti-Jansenist campaign was temporarily replaced by the 'peace of the church', a period of compromise inspired by a more sensitive and tolerant pope.

However, Louis reverted to the persecution of Jansenists in 1679. The death of the duchesse de Longueville removed a powerful protectress of the Jansenists. As we have seen, a 'forward policy' was also adopted towards the Huguenots in the 1680s, and it therefore made sense to repress quasi-heretics as well. Above all, Louis now publicly quarrelled with Rome and was anxious to demonstrate his orthodoxy despite his disagreements with the Pope. The immediate cause of the worsening of relations between the French monarchy and the papacy was the disagreement about the *régale* (see page 35) in which Louis' French opponents were supported by Pope Innocent XI. Louis had only himself to blame for this alliance between some of his own clergy and Rome. His counter-measures such as the Gallican Articles led to the disastrous collapse of French foreign policy; in 1688 Innocent XI decreed the appointment of the anti-French candidate to the vital archbishopric of Cologne. Significantly Colbert de Croissy, Louis' foreign affairs secretary, opined that the Pope must be a Jansenist.

During the last years of his reign, Louis XIV realised that to destroy Jansenism he had to mend his fences with Rome. Therefore in 1693 he disowned the Gallican Articles. French pressure at Rome led to the bull *Vineam Domini* which no longer permitted Jansenists the 'respectful silence' with which since 1668 they had been able to 'pass' on sensitive theological issues. With papal support Louis sent soldiers to expel the remaining nuns from Port-Royal. In 1711 he ordered the buildings to be razed to the ground and the bones of dead Jansenists to be reburied in a common grave. The climax to Louis' war on the Jansenists came with the Pope's bull *Unigenitus* in September 1713, which condemned 101 heretical propositions in Jansenist literature. Now surely Jansenism was dead and buried.

Such was by no means the case. For *Unigenitus* proved to be a misjudgement. In order to condemn Jansenism once and for all, the bull adopted a provocatively authoritarian stance. For instance the laity were forbidden to consult the Bible. The bull provoked sympathy for Jansenists and hostility towards Rome. The *parlement* of Paris only registered *Unigenitus* under protest, while 15 bishops refused to observe it. When he was instructed to discipline the Bishop of Metz, Pontchartrain, the Chancellor, resigned. In order to restore discipline and ensure unanimous acceptance of the bull, Louis proposed to summon a council of the French church over which he himself would preside. But he died first, so Jansenism survived.

At the Rastadt conference in 1714 the French asked Prince Eugene how the authorities in the Empire tackled Jansenism. The Prince replied that he had no idea and that he was astonished that the King of France wasted his time on such obscure matters of theology. It is difficult to disagree with Eugene when weighing up the results of Louis XIV's handling of the Jansenists. Granted, the king had used his authority to protect the orthodoxy of the French Church and nation. But was it worth it? In the pursuit of his goal Louis quarrelled with the papacy, alienated his own clergy and clashed with the Paris *parlement*. Far from being repressed, Jansenists not only survived but had their revenge. When the supreme crisis of the Bourbon monarchy occurred in the summer of 1789, Louis XVI was to be confronted by an alliance between the third estate (the bourgeoisie) and the first estate (the clergy). The first estate was dominated by Jansenist curés. This was the legacy of Louis XIV to his great-great-grandson.

5 Quietism

Quietism was influential in many parts of seventeenth-century Europe, including France. It has a long history. It emphasises the soul's ability to communicate with God. The individual can thus shortcut the more usual forms of worship and instruction; sacraments and sermons are rendered unnecessary. Not surprisingly, Quietism has always been regarded with suspicion by ecclesiastical authorities. Furthermore, by its very nature it has tended to be popular with eccentrics.

Such was Madame Guyon who irrupted onto the French religious scene in June 1687. She was a rich, intense widow and a prolific author. In her book *A Short and Very Easy Way of Praying from the Heart* she advocated total love-surrender to the divine:

1 Our surrender ought to be an entire leaving of ourselves in the
   hands of God, forgetting ourselves in a great measure and thinking
   only on God; by this means only the heart remains always free,
   contented and disengaged. As to the practice of this virtue, it
5 consists in a continued forsaking and losing of self-will in the will of
   God; in renouncing all particular self-inclinations as soon as we
   feel them arise in us, willing only what God from eternity hath
   willed ...

Colbert's daughters introduced this prayer-specialist to Madame de Maintenon. With remarkable naivety she was impressed by Madame Guyon and her doctrines. In fact Madame de Maintenon considered Madame Guyon just the person to raise the spiritual tone at Saint-Cyr, the school which she had founded for the daughters of impoverished noblemen. The girls happened to be in a worryingly excitable state having just performed Racine's play *Esther*. Madame Guyon was therefore commissioned to produce a more prayerful atmosphere. She certainly succeeded. Teachers and pupils were soon 'meditating' by lying on the chapel floor when they should have been in class. Experiencing an ecstatic relationship with the divine was even more fun than *Esther*.

It was Madame de Maintenon's confessor, the Bishop of Chartres, who rumbled Madame Guyon. He knew exactly what to make of her and demanded her dismissal. Madame de Maintenon was convinced by the bishop. When she changed her mind about somebody, she changed it completely. Madame Guyon was thrown into prison and her books were burnt.

Unfortunately, Madame de Maintenon was not the only person to be impressed by Madame Guyon. Perhaps the reign's most charismatic figure was François de Salignac de la Mothe-Fénelon. He too was one of Madame de Maintenon's protegés. On her recommmendation Fénelon had been made tutor to the king's grandson, the duc de Burgundy, and had been appointed to the Archbishopric of Cambrai. Fénelon should have known better than to have fallen for Madame Guyon. But he was charitable, gullible and attracted to mysticism. As Saint-Simon put it, 'their sensitive natures merged'. Even after Madame Guyon had been removed from Saint-Cyr, Fénelon continued to defend her books. His campaign brought him into conflict with the Bishop of Meaux, Jacques-Benigne Bossuet, the defender of the revocation of the Edict of Nantes. The French Church and the court were entertained by a gladiatorial contest between the 'Lion of Meaux' and the 'Swan of Cambrai'. Madame de Maintenon changed her mind about Fénelon as well, so that Bossuet was able to boast: 'We have on our side God, the truth, a worthy motive, the king and Madame de Maintenon'. Against this combination Fénelon could only lose. He was banished to Cambrai, and Madame Guyon's books were finally and unequivocally condemned.

One person who was not impressed by Quietism was Louis XIV. As we have seen, he had no sympathy with any form of religion which was remotely unorthodox. He was furious with Madame de Maintenon, reducing her to tears and banishing her to her room, where she had to stay for months. Grief and worry almost killed her until Louis prompted to mercy by the Bishop of Chartres at last went to his wife's bedside. 'Madame, are you really going to die of this business?' he asked her. She smiled through her tears and they were reconciled. But there was no forgiveness for Fénelon who had to circulate his diocese with a condemnation of his own books. He retaliated by becoming one of Louis' sternest and most eloquent critics.

Why was the king so angry? Perhaps because he himself had been made to look inept, for his wife and one of his favoured churchmen had made exhibitions of themselves. No doubt also he was grieved to see the Church for which he felt himself responsible demean itself while confidence in its teaching was eroded. This point was made by Racine:

> In these combats where the prelates of France seem to seek after truth, one says that hope is being crushed, another replies that it is charity; it is really faith and no-one gives it a thought.

6 Assessment

In his religious policies Louis XIV threw caution to the winds. On the face of it this is surprising, for in general Louis got his results as ruler of France by compromise and cautious realism. When fulfilling his obligations as the Most Christian King, however, Louis saw things in black and white. So he went for broke.

Many have criticised this high-profile, all-or-nothing approach. In particular Louis' persecution of the Huguenots has been condemned as a bad business in which he displayed neither charity nor humility. Some may admire Louis' campaign for Catholic orthodoxy; in an age when his mother 'could not be bothered with talk about grace' and Charles II of England dismissed Catholicism as 'the only religion fit for a gentleman to die in', Louis at least took his Christianity seriously. Others condemn him as a religious bigot. The reader must choose.

If Louis XIV's priorities are a matter of opinion, his achievements are not. Louis failed to achieve his objectives. He failed to eradicate Huguenot heresy, he failed to achieve uniformity by repressing the Jansenists and the Quietists and he failed to stop Fenelon thinking for himself. Nor was Louis XIV wholly convincing as the 'Most Christian King' - not even in France. True, his low rating at the end of the reign was largely due to his disastrous foreign policy and the collapse of the economy. Nevertheless, the following popular rhyme suggests that Louis' religious policies were disliked:

You might, our great King, beheld with awe
Have followed Jesus and his law
And not loved so much his Society.

This criticism of Louis' subservience to the Jesuits is significant. In the same way he alienated public opinion when he called in the Pope to demolish Jansenism.

In the religious context Louis XIV comes across as a poor tactician, for many of his failures were self-inflicted. Often he attempted the impossible, interfering in matters which he did not understand or which he should have left alone. If Saint-Simon called Madame de Maintenon 'the universal governess', 'universal fidget' describes Louis. In his handling of issues such as Jansenism he did more harm than good. Sadly this summarises Louis' religious policies in general. With pure motives he damaged causes which he tried to defend, to say nothing of the suffering which he inflicted on his victims.

Nevertheless, granted the failures of many of Louis XIV's policies but also the limitations within which he operated, there is a certain steadfastness to admire. Louis did govern, he did have ideals, he honoured his obligations as he understood them. As a result France remained a Catholic nation. In a limited but real sense France still is a Catholic nation. For this achievement it is perverse to deny Louis XIV some credit.

Making notes on Louis XIV and Religion

Do not be discouraged if you are unfamiliar with such terms as 'Jansenist', 'Quietist' - or even 'Catholic' and 'Protestant'. Many others are in the same boat. Make your own note.

Having done this, your best tactics will probably be to follow the pattern of this chapter - i.e. make methodical notes on Louis XIV's relations with the Papacy and his campaigns against the Huguenots, the Jansenists and the Quietists. A particular problem is the inter-relation of Louis' dealings with Rome and his other religious projects. It would be a good idea to make a detailed chronological summary specifically devoted to religious affairs.

Examiners sometimes ask if Louis XIV's religious policies were successful. This is a minefield. 'Success' inevitably raises the issue of 'aims': were his aims realistic, did he achieve them? Louis' aim - a regimented, Catholic France - clearly eluded him. Yet in the climate of the times he was surprisingly successful. Make a note on his achievements however incomplete they may have been.

Answering essay questions on *Louis XIV and Religion*

Examiners still concentrate on the revocation of the Edict of Nantes, occasionally broadening the canvas to Louis XIV's treatment of the Huguenots. This is not to say that the material in this chapter on Louis' relations with Rome or his handling of the Jansenist controversy will not be useful to you if you are required to assess Louis' achievement as a whole. You might be asked to evaluate the success of Louis XIV's religious policies - it is after all a good question - although, judging by examiners' past performance, it is not likely.

Anyway, let us be realistic and concentrate on the revocation. Questions tend to be on the causes of Louis XIV's decision or on the consequences. So consider the following:

For what reasons did Louis XIV revoke the Edict of Nantes?

In your introduction explain why this is a historically significant question, given that Louis' campaign against Protestantism was already achieving impressive results and that he was not by nature a cruel or bigoted person. Yet he took this decision which caused immense suffering, irreparably damaged his own reputation and presented his enemies with a propaganda coup. The main body of your essay should be devoted to possible explanations. A paragraph could with profit be allotted to each of the following propositions:
i)   Louis took the decision to revoke because the Edict was no longer needed. Protestantism had virtually disappeared - so he thought.
ii)   Louis took the decision to revoke because pressures were brought to bear on him by his confessors, public opinion and his wife.
iii) Louis revoked because he wanted to impress Catholic Europe and to pull back a few points in his rivalry with the Emperor.
iv)   Louis revoked because he wished to achieve uniformity in France, thus defeating the menace of political and social subversion.
v)   The popularity of the measure proves that public opinion was on Louis' side.

In your conclusion indicate which of these explanations you find most convincing. In addition you could point out that Louis could not predict the future, nor could he know everything about the present. He was badly informed and badly advised - not the first leader in history to be handicapped in this way! Everyone makes mistakes. Or does this amount to excessively kind special pleading on the Sun King's behalf?

Source-based questions on *Louis XIV and Religion*

1 The Persecution of the Huguenots
Carefully read the Proclamation addressed to the Protestants (page 38) and the description of the 'dragonnades' (page 39). Answer the following questions.
a) What did the author of the Proclamation hope to achieve? (3 marks)
b) Were Louis XIV's own priorities and principles more accurately reflected in the Proclamation or in the description of the dragonnades? Explain your answer. (6 marks).
c) How far do these documents justify the description of Louis' treatment of the Huguenots as 'tyranny'? (6 marks)

2 Louis XIV and the Jansenists
Carefully read the account of Archbishop Perefix's attack on the Abbess of Port Royal (page 45) and the criticism of Louis XIV (page 49). Answer the following questions.
a) Why did the archbishop rebuke the abbess? (3 marks)
b) In the second extract, name the Society which Louis XIV was alleged to favour. Why was he criticised for doing so? (3 marks)
c) What light do these documents shed on Louis XIV's reasons for supporting the campaign against the Jansenists? (4 marks)

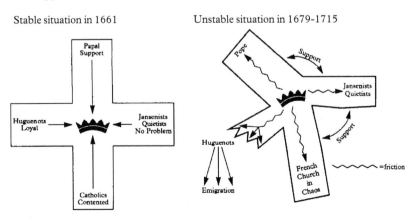

Summary: Louis XIV and Religion

CHAPTER 4

Finance, Taxation and the Economy

1 Background: Economic Facts of Life in 1661

If we are to evaluate the economic policies and achievements of Louis XIV and his ministers, we must establish the parameters within which they operated. What sort of a country was France during the personal rule? What were the problems facing the French people? Were the government's priorities right? What opportunities existed for achieving improvements? How much room for manoeuvre was there?

The first point to make is that the seventeenth century was a time of economic decay for the whole of Europe. Prices and wages fell, there was a shortage of coin and investment, and populations declined. This recession certainly hit France; the population was greater in 1600 than in 1700 and gross national product fell by about 5 per cent during the century. Therefore the picture of a happy, thriving nation that propagandists gave was deceptive. While it is dangerous to generalise about a period before detailed statistics were kept, the French economy would probably have been in trouble whatever the government had done.

The most striking fact was that France had difficulty feeding herself. With eighteen and a half million inhabitants the country was more heavily populated than most states in Europe; contemporary England, Scotland and Wales, for example, had a population of six million. Yet much of France consists of fertile soil which, combined with a benign climate, should easily have fed the population. In practice this did not happen. Most French people lived on or below subsistence level, while starvation inevitably resulted from especially bad harvests. Because there was little food in reserve, hunger and the threat of hunger made the Sun King's reign a nightmare for most of his people.

Why was this the case? Part of the explanation was the parlous state of French agriculture. The peasantry was locked in a vicious cycle of poor crops and poor soil. Because the demand for grain was so acute in order to provide bread for an impoverished population, there was excessive concentration on arable farming. This caused a shortage of animals which in its turn meant ineffectually propelled ploughs and a lack of manure. Shallow ploughing and inadequate fertilising combined with soil exhaustion to produce poor yields which caused poverty and the inability to buy animals. So it went on.

What were peasants to do in such desperate circumstances? Some simply starved or succumbed to the diseases which accompany malnutrition. Others left their homes to join the ever-increasing bands of vagrants which terrorised the countryside; or they tried their luck in the towns. The commonest reaction was to get into debt. There were always wealthier peasants, landlords or middle-class investors in the local town who were glad to lend to destitute peasants with the prospect of acquiring their property if the loan was not repaid. It will be appreciated that these short-term reactions to economic disaster were bound to cause ever-increasing long-term problems: more and more landless debtors, more and more beggars and destitute drifters thronging the nation's inadequate and overcrowded poorhouses.

The government's regulations for the control of Paris's vagrants indicate official attitudes:

1 As there were no general poorhouses for shutting up the poor and for punishing able-bodied but idle beggars, the Paris house has received a large number of paupers from other towns and provinces who presented themselves at its gates. We have therefore
5 thought it reasonable to regulate on the one hand the kinds of people who must be received and looked after charitably inside this poorhouse, and on the other hand to create new penalties which will make a rather stronger impact on these vagabonds. To this end we order that there shall be freely received into this Poorhouse of
10 our great city of Paris all poor children and the aged of either sex, those suffering from epilepsy, fits and other ills of this nature ... We further order that all able-bodied persons of either sex, and over sixteen years old, who have the necessary strength to gain their own livelihood, shall be confined in separate buildings for each sex
15 where they shall be given only what is absolutely necessary for their existence, and shall be employed on the harshest work which their bodies will support.

The satirist Jonathan Swift suggested, with tongue in cheek, that the children of such unfortunates should be killed and marketed as food. The French authorities' reactions might seem to be almost as callous. Yet the poor laboured under still greater burdens.

In Louis XIV's France taxation was levied on the principle that those who could afford least paid most. On top of all the handicaps imposed by nature and unsympathetic authorities came the demands of the landlord, the priest and the government's tax-collector. During Louis' reign rents and tolls demanded by the local seigneur became more onerous because they were not lowered to conform to falling wages. Tithe, amounting on average to about 11 per cent of all produce, was a long-established obligation whereby in theory the parish priest was maintained by his parishioners; in practice most of the money collected went to some distant abbey or wealthy bishop. Meanwhile, the government exacted the *taille* (a crude land tax imposed on the poor) and purchase taxes such as the *gabelle* (a tax on salt which was an absolute necessity of life). During the wars in which France had been involved under the cardinals the taxation of the peasantry had been raised to what was considered to be the highest practicable limit. Yet

Louis XIV's wars caused a further increase of 50 per cent. The consequences were national impoverishment and the ruin of the peasants.

The contrast between France and England is instructive. While contemporary England was not exactly a compassionate society, landlords were prepared to spend money on improvements. They were keen to invest in new breeds of animals and new farming techniques. There was a lively literature on the subject. In France on the other hand there was no literature and no investment. Both aristocrats and townsfolk were prepared to buy land, but they clearly did not see any need to maximise the profits to be made from their purchase - they were content with the social standing that its ownership gave them. Instead they joined the tax-farmers or lent money to the government at high rates of interest or purchased offices (salaried posts often involving minimal duties which governments were reduced to selling in order to stay solvent). What they did not do was invest in agricultural improvements. As a result, peasants were given no stimulus by go-ahead rivals, no financial support from their landlords if they were tenants and no opportunity to improve their own property since all their surplus income was absorbed by taxation.

Is this too gloomy a picture? Of course the pattern varied. Crops were unlikely to fail all over France at one time - though communications were so abysmal that it was difficult for the fortunate to supply the unfortunate. Some parts of France escaped crop failures completely, if they were lucky with soil and weather; others such as the *Massif Central* suffered permanent recession. Perhaps in a rudimentary way the village operated as a community, looking after its poor in times of crisis. No doubt peasants themselves learnt to survive the hard way. To avoid having children they could not afford they married late or practised rudimentary birth-control. However, historians are convinced that conditions on the land were terrible. How peasants survived, how they paid taxes, why they did not rebel more often, are good questions.

When we turn to the towns the position was almost as depressing. Most French towns in Louis XIV's reign were basically parasitical, living off and exploiting the local peasantry, the urban bourgeoisie frequently buying property at knock-down prices. Only Paris with maybe 400,000 and Lyon with 100,000 would rank today as major cities. Sea-ports such as Marseille, Bordeaux and St. Malo were genuine trading centres. However, the majority of towns were merely provincial capitals, the seats of bishops or overgrown villages dominated by the local nobility, inhabited by petty traders and craftsmen within the walls and impoverished vagrants in shanty-settlements outside. Manufacture was impeded by the restrictive practices of the guilds, as was internal trade by countless local tolls and regulations. France was not fundamentally a trading or a manufacturing nation. Only 10 per cent of the population were not employed on the land and of these the majority produced cheap clothing and equipment for peasants. Most manufacturing and marketing businesses were on a small scale. Merchants who prospered were quick to buy their way into the official classes, abandoning trade for a more socially acceptable existence.

For seventeenth-century France was deeply snobbish. Everyone admired and envied the nobles who had their recognisable lifestyle to which they were entitled and which they were obliged to maintain. They were not allowed to demean themselves by participating in trade. Even estate-management which their English contemporaries regarded as socially acceptable was for a French nobleman inferior to the only truly aristocratic activities - the court, the Church and the army. After all, it was in recognition of his service to the State on the battlefield that the nobleman was exempt from the payment of *taille*. There was no greater cause of France's economic backwardness than this prejudice against involvement in business and industry. The leaders of society and the nation's best minds turned their backs on the problems of national deficits, moribund trade and the frequent inability to feed France's millions satisfactorily. And when Louis' personal rule began, these problems were getting worse, not better.

This was largely because the Crown had made its own contribution to France's economic difficulties. As we have seen, France's involvement in war was paid for by taxing the peasants to the uttermost. When this source was exhausted, the crown borrowed at high interest, using future tax yields as security. The other chief source of revenue was the sale of office. No less than 45,000 posts were created in order to be sold, thus perpetuating an inefficient, hereditary and costly bureaucracy. Here were classic examples of short-term expedients creating long-term problems; the need for ready cash triumphed over prudent house-keeping. Thus the cardinals left the Crown saddled with crippling debts, mortgaged revenue and an army of unproductive office-holders. Inevitably the Crown's difficulties were passed on to the peasant tax-payers who picked up the bill for their masters' follies.

So to be fair to Louis XIV and the men he put in charge of the economy, the prospects for a happy and prosperous reign in 1661 were poor. A wise ruler would have concentrated on avoiding war, breaking down prejudices against trade and drastically improving French agriculture. But it is easy to say this with hindsight; Louis had other and seemingly more pressing priorities even though France did indeed have serious economic problems when his personal rule began.

2 The Career, Policies and Achievements of Colbert, 1661-83

Between 1661 and his death in 1683 the French economy was dominated by Jean-Baptiste Colbert. This formidable and efficient administrator has provoked controversy. Until recently historians have admired him both as a man and as a statesman. They have warmed to his supposedly middle-class background, his dedicated approach and his opposition to the persecution of the Huguenots. Above all they have compared Colbert's belief in *le bon sense* with Louvois' pursuit of *la gloire* - the peaceful priorities of the one contrasting with the bellicose tendencies of the other. Indeed, Louvois has been depicted as Louis XIV's evil genius who progressively supplanted Colbert as the dominating influence over the Sun King; Colbert's death was allegedly a disaster both for Louis XIV and for France. Recently, however, it has been suggested that this picture is oversimplified. Colbert's policies and achievements have been harshly criticised, while a case has been made both for Louvois and for Colbert's successors as managers of the French economy. Where does the truth lie?

Certainly there was nothing saintly about Colbert's rise to power. His success was due to luck, ability and the use of his elbows. Colbert's humble origins have been exaggerated as his uncle had been a senior official in the war office and Le Tellier's brother-in-law. Indeed, Colbert was originally a protégé of the Le Tellier faction. However, his career really took off when his talents were spotted by Mazarin and it was as the cardinal's 'creature' that Colbert came to the king's notice. Before Mazarin's death Colbert was already working for the king, looking after his mistresses and his bastards. Colbert was, in Mazarin's opinion, his most precious bequest to Louis XIV - discreet, effective and loyal. The day before the cardinal died, Colbert was named *intendant des finances*. This was an influential position, although Colbert was still subordinate to the *surintendant*, Nicholas Fouquet. Colbert's progress depended on Fouquet's disgrace.

Colbert was well-placed to bring down Fouquet, who had managed Mazarin's fortune. This had grown from very little when the cardinal returned from exile to 35 million livres at his death. Colbert knew that this fortune was made at the expense of the state and that Fouquet was also enriching himself. In the event, Fouquet made Colbert's task easier. First, he offended the king. He clearly believed that Louis' decision to be his own first minister was not to be taken seriously and that he himself would soon be the cardinal's successor. Meanwhile Fouquet's *parvenu* (upstart) ostentation and his affairs with noblemen's wives made him many enemies. In August 1661 he entertained the court with tactless splendour at his new house, Vaux le Vicomte. A few days later he was arrested.

Fouquet's trial was managed by Colbert with a vindictive disregard for justice. The accusation that he had fortified Belle-Isle to defy the king was patently absurd, just as the charge that he had defrauded the state was patently correct. However, Fouquet cleverly implicated both the dead Mazarin and Colbert. One of the judges successfully argued that in these circumstances the death penalty would be unjust - and thereby ruined his own career; Colbert saw to that. A sentence of banishment was 'commuted' by the king to solitary life imprisonment in the fortress of Pinerolo where Fouquet eventually died in 1680.

However, Colbert's campaign to ruin Fouquet was not entirely based on ambition and malice; the king's best interests influenced him too. Colbert was in favour of solving the indebtedness of the Crown by a declaration of bankruptcy, with a *chambre de justice* being set up to investigate the sharp practices of financiers who had lent money to the Crown and abused their position. On the other hand, Fouquet believed that to default on the Crown's debts and set up a *chambre de justice* would alienate the financial establishment whose support the Crown needed. Louis decided to back Colbert. He was glad of the opportunity to demonstrate that no-one was immune from royal justice. In addition, he shared the aristocracy's resentment of Fouquet's presumption. Furthermore, given the unpopularity of the previous régime, Fouquet served as a scapegoat, while the Crown's debts to Fouquet were cancelled and his fortune acquired at a stroke. Meanwhile, by no means all the financiers were alienated, for Colbert convinced them that it was in their interests to serve the Crown.

Louis XIV was right to back Colbert, for he was just the man he needed. Colbert saw his role as *intendant des finances* very simply. He was the king's servant. He accepted Louis' indifference to the economic welfare of the realm, the prosperity of the French people and the distribution of taxation. France was the king's estate. Colbert was the king's estate-manager whose duty it was to find the money for the king's policies. The king concentrated his mind on war and foreign policy, which inevitably were expensive. Their success depended on Colbert's expertise. Although Louis had a disconcerting habit of requiring 'all the details', in truth he had little interest in how Colbert raised the money provided that it was there when he needed it.

Louis showed his appreciation of Colbert's loyalty and efficiency. After Fouquet's fall Colbert joined Le Tellier and Lionne as members of the inner council. In 1665 Louis made Colbert Controller-General of the Finances, and in 1669 secretary for the navy and the royal household. From 1664 Colbert directed Louis' building projects and patronage of the arts. He retained these posts - as well as Louis' confidence and support - until his death. Because the king recognised Colbert's loyalty, he had no objection to him enriching himself. In fact Louis encouraged this and when Colbert's daughters married dukes, Louis himself contributed to their dowries.

Colbert brought immense application to his task, usually working 15 hours a day. His austere dedication to duty earned him the nickname 'the north wind' - due to the icy blast of his displeasure with slackers or crooks. His approach was methodical. Every month he presented the king with a summary of the financial situation, and at the end of the year with a statement of income and expenditure, plus estimates for the coming year. Colbert conducted frequent enquiries, obliging the *intendants* to submit statistics with regard to population, taxation and productive capacity of their localities. This concern for clear information was perhaps Colbert's chief claim to originality. It was much appreciated by his bureaucratic master.

When it came to directing the French economy, Colbert's policies were conservative. He was influenced by the mercantilist ideas of the time: a state should amass gold by boosting exports, limiting imports and prohibiting the movement of gold out of the country. Colbert seems to have accepted that just as the amount of precious metal in circulation was limited, so were the opportunities to trade and profit. Logically, therefore, a nation could only improve its balance of trade by beggaring its neighbours. In effect this meant that France could only prosper by defeating foreign rivals such as the Dutch and the English.

Colbert appreciated the importance of the leaders of society setting an example. Whereas in Holland the ruling oligarchs were rich merchants, in France the nobles snobbishly refused to participate in trade. Colbert therefore persuaded the king to legislate in 1669:

1 Seeing that commerce, and particularly that which goes by sea, is
  the fertile source from which states draw their wealth, that there is
  no more lawful and blameless means of acquiring wealth, and also
  that it has always been held in high regard by the best ordered
5 nations, and is universally welcomed as one of the most
  honourable occupations in civil life ... we do say and declare that it
  is our wish and pleasure that all gentlemen be permitted to join
  companies for, and take part in the building of merchant ships and
  trading in, the goods which they carry, without being censored for
10 so doing and without it being claimed that they have forfeited the
  status of nobility, provided that they on no occasion participate in
  retail trading.

Not surprisingly Colbert also had a low opinion of the Church's refusal to pull its weight. Grimly observing that 'there are no monks in Holland', he ordered the monasteries to produce cloth.

What did Colbert actually achieve? He was at his most impressive in the context of state finance. He ensured that the Crown received much more of the money which was collected by the tax-farmers than had previously been the case; the annual cost of collecting the revenue were reduced from 52 million livres to 24 million. Investigations and prosecutions created a climate in which men were less keen to attempt to swindle the Crown. Several noblemen who claimed tax-exemption on account of their status were proved to be frauds and had to pay. Colbert reduced the net yield of the *taille* from 42 million livres a year to 35 million as he was aware of the harm done by impoverishing the peasants. He derived more from indirect taxation which continued to hit the poor but at least obliged the rich to pay something. By 1672 the yield from indirect taxation had increased from 36 million livres a year to 62 million. The hated *gabelle* alone brought in 4 million livres more than previously because its collection was improved. Colbert reduced the payments to office-holders and succeeded in borrowing from newly-formed syndicates of financiers at only five per cent. Royal lands which had been sold by Colbert's predecessors were recovered and the financial yield quadrupled between 1661 and 1672. By that date the national budget showed an annual surplus.

It was to strengthen the French economy that Colbert intervened in the spheres of commerce and industry. He believed that by exporting her products France could acquire gold and silver. Conversely, members of the wealthy classes who purchased foreign luxuries were depriving the country of precious metals. The answer therefore was for the state to encourage the development of domestic production. In 1665 Colbert founded the Van Robais woollen factory at Abbeville which employed 2,000 people by the year 1700, the largest industrial business in France. He helped the textile merchants of Languedoc to oust English and Dutch merchants from the Levant by appointing inspectors to raise standards and by eliminating the duties which had impeded Marseille's trade. He subsidised lace making at Auxerre in Burgundy and silk production at Lyon. The Gobelins tapestry and Savonnerie carpet businesses were encouraged by royal patronage. Foreign craftsmen were bribed to settle in France and teach their skills to Frenchmen; the king's envoys in Sweden, Bohemia and the Dutch republic were particularly active in persuading manufacturers of luxury goods to accept the Sun King's patronage. Protective tariffs were introduced, some of the restrictive practices of the guilds, in Lyon for example, were abolished, and monopolistic privileges were awarded for new methods of preparing leather and the manufacture of glass.

Colbert accepted the contemporary opinion that a state was strengthened by trade and should therefore intervene. Four trading companies were founded by royal command - the East India Company (1664), the West Indies Company (1664), the Northern Company (1669), and the Levant Company (1670). Royal capital had to subsidise these enterprises as it proved impossible to persuade private individuals to invest; not even Louis XIV could sell the idea to his courtiers despite his argument that to invest in the East India Company did not count as 'trade' because it led to the spreading of the gospel. As trading ventures the companies were disappointing. The most promising was the East India Company which established centres at Surinat and Pondicherry but never competed effectively with its firmly-established Dutch and English rivals. On the other hand, private enterprise followed Colbert's lead and the number of individual merchants trading overseas rose sharply from 329 in 1664 to 648 in 1704.

Furthermore Colbert's emphasis on matters maritime stimulated the domestic economy. As a result of his development of the navy, ship-building was subsidised, forests were planted and foreign sailors were encouraged to settle in France. Rochefort and Brest, where Colbert established naval arsenals, became thriving ports. The navy's demands for guns and iron fittings to reinforce ships' hulls stimulated the metallurgical industries in Limousin and Dauphiné.

Colbert's economic policies also achieved lasting results overseas. He imposed orderly government on France's colonies in the West Indies and Canada, where there were 15,000 French settlers by 1713; to this day much of Canada's Quebec province is French-speaking. Colbert encouraged exploration for trading purposes, both to develop the Canadian fur trade and to open up the Mississippi further south. Thus Frenchmen were encouraged to think globally and the nation's maritime tradition was established. French merchant ships abounded in the Baltic, the Mediterranean, the Caribbean and the Far East and the French flag waved over the Mississippi and the Ganges.

Colbert tried hard to improve conditions for internal trade. He appreciated the importance of communications. 600,000 livres were spent on the improvement of roads. He was also persuaded that a wise investment by the state would be in the *Canal des Deux Mers* which linked Bordeaux with the Mediterranean; the tax-payer contributed 7,500,000 livres. A postal system with 800 post offices was created and a determined attempt was made to eradicate the numerous internal tolls and tariffs which inhibited the movement of trade. He achieved some success in 1664 by simplifying the tolls levied in the *cinq grosse ferms*, a customs area in the northern provinces of France.

But a more ambitious measure of 1667 which was designed to simplify customs dues on all imports and exports for the whole kingdom proved difficult to enforce; too many local entrepreneurs were making a profit out of the existing arrangements. Similarly Colbert merely provoked resentment by trying to rationalise the different systems of weights and measures which still existed in France; for example 100 livres on Parisian scales equalled 123.5 in Marseille and 120.5 in Avignon, Toulouse and Montpellier. State action of this kind infuriated merchants who argued that unnecessary confusion would be caused by the changes, and so Colbert withdrew most of these instructions.

Nevertheless, Colbert's achievements are to be respected. He was highly effective in raising money for the king. His campaign to eradicate waste, corruption and inefficiency terrified the idle and the crooked. While he failed to convince his fellow-countrymen that France's absurd system of regulations and tolls should be abolished, his attempts to galvanise French trade and industry achieved real, if limited, progress.

3 An Analysis of Colbert's Failures

However, when Colbert died in 1683 it was apparent just how limited his successes were. There was little to show for all his efforts. The

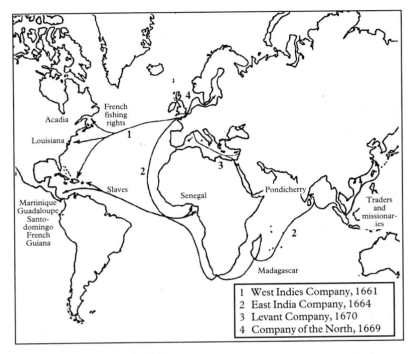

French expansion, 1661-1715

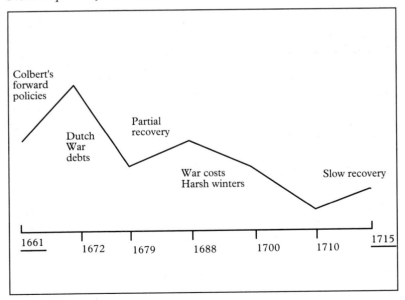

The Economy, 1661-1715

French economy was still backward and the Crown was bankrupt again. What had gone wrong? Had he been undermined or was he to blame?

Colbert's greatest problem was the Dutch. He was driven to distraction by France's inability to compete. Everything the French tried to do, the Dutch did better. Everywhere French industrialists and merchants turned, there were the Dutch. When Colbert protected French producers by imposing tariffs, the Dutch retaliated, and the resulting tariff war did more harm to the French than to the Dutch. Attempts to found colonies and to establish a healthy French mercantile marine found the Dutch already in possession of the vantage points. French traders were persistently undercut by their Dutch rivals who had an infuriating habit of selling at a loss so as to corner the market.

So Colbert concluded that maybe the only answer was to declare war on the United Provinces, invade Holland and either destroy Dutch industry and commerce or take it over. Historians argue about Colbert's responsibility for the Dutch war which Louis XIV unleashed in the summer of 1672. Not that Louis needed much encouragement to attack the presumptuous republic. But Colbert certainly failed to support Lionne, the secretary for foreign affairs, who opposed the war.

The Dutch war destroyed everything that Colbert stood for. The conflict dragged on until the disappointing and unsatisfactory peace of Nymegen in 1679 (see page 103); every day saw the French economy in deeper trouble. Balanced budgets and annual surpluses became things of the past; the Crown was again in debt. Money had to be borrowed at 10 per cent from Genoese bankers and future revenues had to be mortgaged as in the bad old days. Subsidies could no longer be afforded for Colbert's pet projects. The *Manufacture Royale de Beauvais*, having received 175,000 livres between 1665 and 1673, was given nothing between 1674 and 1678. The infant colony of Canada had received financial support from the French government for ten years, but in 1673 was told that from now on it would have to achieve its own salvation. The trading companies were soon in desperate trouble, the Company of the North sending its last ship in 1684. Meanwhile, the king's ever-swelling armies wrecked the prosperity of the provinces where they were billeted, while at the centre of government the longer the war lasted the more ground Colbert lost to his rival, Louvois, the secretary for war. Foreign trade was interrupted by Dutch men-of-war, which were assisted by French merchants' defiance of Colbert's instruction to proceed in convoy. His prohibition of trade between Britanny and the Dutch enemy provoked a full-scale rebellion in 1675.

However, it was not only in wartime that the French refused to be regimented. Colbert believed that France was a unity, that it had a future as a unified economy and that the nation's welfare depended on national prosperity. He therefore felt justified as the king's minister in imposing central direction on the economy. But he utterly failed to convert most Frenchmen to his own beliefs. Was France basically an economic unit? Most Frenchmen were more concerned with the prosperity of their own district. Colbert lacked the imagination and the sensitivity to perceive that Frenchmen living in Bordeaux or St. Malo were more interested in the prosperity of their own locality than of France as a whole. Indeed, from their point of view was there such a thing, in economic terms, as France? If the answer was no, then Colbert's attempts to subordinate local to national interests could only provoke resentment and defiance in provincial France.

Several examples can be quoted of provincial refusal to comply with Colbert's interventionist policies. At Marseille the merchants preferred to use their silver and gold to buy imports from the Levant rather than investing in the export of French goods. At Beauvais Colbert's regulations for the production of tapestries and fine linen were ignored. Local tariff barriers remained because the provincial oligarchies profited from them, just as the guilds defied Colbert's attempts to abolish their privileges. Roger Mettam has written, 'The only indication that there had once been a minister, Jean-Baptiste Colbert, who had tried to rationalise and expand the economy of the kingdom, was to be found in the wariness shown by these local élites towards every government pronouncement on economic matters'.

Where there was progress, it was usually because local interests were consulted. Thus when the East India Company was formed, the Archbishop of Lyon persuaded the local merchants to invest 1,000,000 livres on condition that according to their wishes the headquarters should be located in their city. Again, the *Canal des Deux Mers* was constructed because Pierre Paul Riquet, the local millionaire, and the Archbishop of Toulouse were won round first. Colbert never appreciated that projects lacking local support and enthusiasm would fail.

Colbert's campaign to mobilise support for his progressive ideas was also defeated by class prejudices. This problem began at the top. It took Colbert nineteen years to persuade Louis XIV to visit a naval arsenal. When Colbert assembled 'the 150 girls, the mares, the stallions, the lambs that we have to send to Canada', the king made objections, forbidding Huguenot emigration for example. No wonder the aristocracy took their cue from the Crown, staunchly resisting Colbert's encouragement to show interest in commerce. In their turn office-holders set their sights on nobility, rather than investing in the new economic opportunities, while successful merchants preferred to invest in office rather than develop their businesses.

Colbert's bossy authoritarianism was ultimately counter-productive. He complained that the French were idle. But who could blame noblemen who reflected that if they complied with Colbert's instruction to invest in seaborne trade, they would lose their noble status the next time he held an enquiry into tax-evasion? Colbert believed that the only way the French could win was through state direction. But while he could order criminals to be moved from the gaols where they were useless to the galleys where under the lash they could be useful, it was not so easy to regiment the rest of society.

Colbert's insensitivity was matched by economic blindness. He failed to appreciate that the backbone of the French economy was agriculture. Many of his policies actually damaged the peasants, for example his withdrawal of the low quality copper coinage on which their trade depended. Or again, in the interests of the navy's need for timber, Colbert drove the peasants out of the forests. If he showed interest in the breeding of horses this was purely for military purposes. He lowered the *taille* - but that was so that the peasants could pay promptly. Otherwise Colbert was as indifferent to agriculture and the welfare of the vast majority of the population as was his royal master. Instead of subsidising luxury industries and non-viable trading companies, he should have invested in agricultural research - or in the manufacture of cheap, low quality products which French people could afford. But unfortunately with all his qualities, Colbert lacked the grasp of reality to achieve greater success.

4 The French Economy after Colbert, 1683-1715

It is a tribute to Colbert that the development of the French economy during the reign of Louis XIV should be so linked with his name. Yet when Colbert died, the personal rule still had 32 years to run; furthermore during the period 1683 to 1715 the French economy by no means stood still. Certainly Colbert's successors adopted a lower profile; they were less ambitious, less domineering, not such all-rounders as the great Controller-General had been. It must be conceded that Chamillart who could give the king a good game of billiards was a bad Controller General (1699-1708) but he was the exception. Louis' other appointments were by no means the disasters that old-fashioned textbooks have suggested. France was confronted with colossal economic problems during the later years of the reign. These problems provoked some interesting and worthwhile responses. Indeed research has proved that in many ways Colbert's successors were his superiors.

He was immediately followed by Louvois, who to a great extent pursued similar policies - the same attempts to direct the national economy from the centre, the same incentives offered to favoured undertakings in the shape of privileges and monopolies, the same frustrations at the dragging of provincial feet. The general instructions for dyers which Colbert had issued in 1671 contained 371 clauses; in 1688 they were reissued with 416. Louvois imposed regulations for the sowing of woad: 'The seed is to be sown in the last quarter of the moon in February or the first quarter of the moon in March and at all the full moons until the month of May'. Furthermore, France swarmed with snoopers who tried to ensure that such regulations were observed.

The one major departure from Colbertian principles was the persecution of the Huguenots. Madame de Maintenon reported that Louvois 'accepted the idea more readily than M. Colbert who thinks only about financial matters and rarely ever about religion'. Colbert had indeed argued for generous treatment of these useful people. Louvois, on the other hand, has always been associated with the opposite policy which was implemented after Colbert's death and reached its climax in the revocation of the Edict of Nantes in October 1685 (see page 40).

What were the economic consequences of this policy of persecution? Protestant propagandists have emphasised the damage to the French economy which resulted. They have understandably presented a story of well-merited retribution for mindless intolerance. However, historians have recently questioned whether the persecution in general and the revocation in particular made much difference. France suffered from the economic malaise which affected the whole of Europe. It is difficult to prove therefore that the persecution of Huguenots was a major cause of the fall in population of between one and three million which occurred in seventeenth-century France, or of the recession in industry, or of the decline in agricultural production which led to lower standards of living. Even so, contemporaries certainly thought that the persecution disrupted trade, damaged the property market and impeded recruitment for the navy. While such industries as Lyon silk had been declining long before the 1680s, the emigration of 200,000 talented and industrious Protestants cannot have helped such industries as textiles and glass-blowing, though they were replaced by Catholic refugees from Ireland and Scotland.

The death of Louvois in 1691 was a watershed in French economic policy. Some of Colbert's most treasured assumptions were now questioned. The merits of free trade were canvassed, as was the case for less government interference rather than more. Colbert's successors set up a *conseil de commerce* in 1700; this differed from the councils of bureaucrats which had dictated to the mercantile community in Colbert's time. Many of its members were merchants. The government now realised that it could help industry and trade by consulting those actively involved. As a result during the war of the Spanish Succession French merchants were allowed to continue to trade with the enemy, especially with England and Scotland.

Colbert's conservatism was jettisoned in the realm of state finance. In 1694 Vauban, one of France's best and most thoughtful generals, advocated the imposition of an income tax of 7 per cent without exceptions. This revolutionary idea was prompted by the acute financial crisis of that year which was caused by the combination of war taxation and harvest failure. Controller-General Pontchartrain (1689-99) could not quite go this far, but in the following year he imposed a *capitation* or poll tax. This was a most significant and interesting experiment. The population was divided into 22 classes according to their ability to pay. The richest paid 2,000 livres a head, the poorest one livre. The tax caused a great furore, too many privileged people managed to evade it, and the *intendants* despaired of collecting it. The yield of 22 million livres in the first year was disappointing. The tax was lifted when peace was made in 1697 but was revived in 1702 when war broke out again. By introducing this radical measure, which was a real attempt to break down the outrageous injustice of the Bourbon tax system, Pontchartrain had shown himself to be more far-sighted than Colbert. And at the same time he proved that he had orthodox ability as well by reducing the taille during the period between the wars (1697-1702) and reducing payment on the *rentes* from 8.5 per cent to 5 per cent.

Desmarets (1708-15) was similarly resourceful during the crisis of 1710 caused by famine and enemy invasion. He introduced the *dixième*. This was the first example of an income tax in European history. Furthermore it was deducted at source. Again, mass evasion, deals whereby men bought themselves out by one usually inadequate payment, and rebellions against the tax-collectors reduced the efficacy of this modern-sounding tax. Nevertheless, the *capitation* and the *dixième* doubled the yield of direct taxation - a remarkable achievement.

Yet although, in financial administration as in other spheres, war proved to be the mother of invention, the difficulties created by the costs of the wars between 1688 and 1713 were so horrendous that in truth no-one, conservative or radical, possessed of however much genius or wizardry, could have found a satisfactory solution. And how could any minister have rescued a master who continued to spend 600,000 livres a year on the Jacobite court at Saint-Germain? As one historian has remarked, 'to impossibilities were added absurdities'. The story of the French economy in the last years of Louis XIV's reign is one long disaster. Devaluation and the creation of paper money combined with frenetic borrowing and sale of office could only postpone the total bankruptcy which prevailed at the Sun King's death. Despite all the expedients adopted, including the most ruthless taxation yet, the Crown's debt stood at 2,300 million livres in 1715.

The seriousness of the situation even affected Louis XIV. No longer did he regard financial ruin as an acceptable feature of the aristocratic way of life; not ruin of such enormity, causing such widespread suffering, to say nothing of such unpopularity for the king and his family. During the severe winter of 1708-9 the Dauphin was mobbed by starving townsfolk in Versailles, while Madame de Maintenon did not dare leave her rooms. Despite the fact that Louis responded by melting down some of the treasures in his palace, he was viciously and widely lampooned for his selfishness and incompetence.

Undoubtedly the privileged classes from the king downwards were still cushioned against hardship. Indeed, financiers such as the ex-Huguenot Samuel Bernard made colossal fortunes out of France's crises. There was never any shortage of rentiers glad to purchase yet more offices. 'Every time Your Majesty creates an office, God creates a fool to buy it', Pontchartrain said to the king. But were they fools? To secure a government pension plus the social respectability of being an office-holder was obviously considered a good return for an investment. Ultimately such people might even achieve noble status and become totally exempt from regular taxation.

For it was the unprivileged poor who paid. And they paid despite famine, destitution and death. In the forests around Versailles children resorted to cannibalism. Peasants dined off Sunday 'joints' consisting of congealed blood drawn from their starving beasts. In 1694 Fénelon, the Archbishop of Cambrai, wrote a hard-hitting letter to Louis XIV and, although the king probably never saw it, nevertheless it remains a valid contemporary comment:

1 Meanwhile your people whom you should have loved as your children and who have hitherto been so devoted to you are dying of hunger. The cultivation of the soil is almost completely abandoned; the cities and the countryside are depopulated; all industry is 5 stagnant; it no longer offers workmen employment. All commerce has been decimated. You have thus consumed half the real wealth and vitality of your kingdom in order to wage war and defend vain conquests abroad. Rather than squeezing money from the poor people, you ought to give them alms and nourish them. The whole 10 of France is little more than a great poorhouse, desolate and with no provisions ... This, Sire, is the state of things. You live as one whose eyes are fatally blinded.

Historians point out that Fénelon was not an impartial observer (he had been disgraced by the king), that the economic problems of France were by no means all Louis' fault, and that some parts of France remained prosperous. Nevertheless, the evidence is there to justify the description of France as a 'great poorhouse' - and the main reason was the taxation necessitated by Louis XIV's wars.

Perhaps the truth is that the economic policies and achievements of Louis XIV and his ministers made relatively little difference. The difficulties of making any impression on such a huge and ungovernable country rendered any initiative ineffectual. Thus throughout the reign in all probability more goods were smuggled into France than came through the customs. Add the determination of the majority of merchants and businessmen not to be regimented by anyone, least of all some bureaucrat in Paris hundreds of miles away, plus the social and economic anomalies which were so in-built that only a revolution could shift them, and one is amazed that Colbert and his successors achieved anything apart from the extraction of money from the tax-payer.

Sadly there is no evidence that these capable and intelligent men identified the correct priorities; still less did they succeed in taking appropriate action. Thus the scandalously unjust system of taxation continued to favour the rich at the expense of the poor. French agriculture still languished, backward and starved of investment. French trade was still impeded by countless tolls and regulations. The Crown was saddled with vast debts and hordes of useless office-holders. Louis XIV's failure to address these problems bequeathed ruin to his successors.

Making notes on Finance, Taxation and the Economy

Examiners tend to ask questions mainly about Colbert. However, you would be well advised to broaden your approach to include the economic achievement of the reign as a whole. For one thing, your answer on Colbert will be enriched by efficient knowledge of the consequences of both his policies and those of his successors. And who knows, you might get a question on the economy during the whole reign.

In your notes identify France's economic problems during the personal rule. Then summarise Colbert's rise to power and his basic attitude to the economy; was he a Mercantilist? You need to follow this with a summary of his achievements, his failures and the reasons for his failures. A review of developments after Colbert's death will place his achievements in perspective. Use the arguments in the chapter to formulate your own conclusion on Colbert's success or failure.

You should also summarise the economic aspect of the revocation of the Edict of Nantes. Examiners occasionally ask questions specifically on this topic. But in any case a well-organised note will equip you to give depth to your answers on other topics besides the economy.

Answering essay questions on Finance, Taxation and the Economy

Here again examiners tend to concentrate on one particular aspect of the story - the policies, achievements and mistakes of Colbert. As you will have noted from reading the text, this is a bizarre state of affairs as Colbert died before the personal rule reached the half-way stage. However, 'ours not to reason why'. And a good grasp of the whole economic history of the reign will broaden your answers on other topics, such as an assessment of the Sun King's record as a whole.
Consider the following questions:
1 Did Colbert revolutionise the French economy?
2 'Colbert served his king well, France less well'. Do you agree?
3 Were the priorities of Colbert's economic policies the right ones?
4 How successful was Colbert in his management of the French economy?

5   Is it fair to describe Colbert as a mercantilist?
6   Why was Colbert not more successful in his economic policies?
Also be prepared for:
7   Discuss the economic consequences of the revocation of the Edict of
    Nantes.
8   Discuss the economic consequences for France of Louis XIV's
    aggressive foreign policy.
9   Was France stronger or weaker economically at the end of the
    personal rule of Louis XIV than she had been at the beginning?

Let us now concentrate on the questions relating to Colbert's success or
failure - the most probable slants of all if there is a question on Colbert in
your paper. When answering questions asking you how successful
Colbert was, the introduction is absolutely crucial. You must establish
what Colbert's aims were: the provision of money for the king, the
encouragement of French trade and industry, and the development of
France as a naval and imperial power. Similarly, if you are asked to
explain why Colbert was not more successful, you must establish in your
introduction how successful he was; list his failures with regard to the
attitudes of the governing class, the refusal of French merchants and
producers to be managed, and the continuing backwardness of French
agriculture. These are classic examples of questions where you will never
recover from a muddled start. Once you have established what Colbert's
aims were or what his failures amounted to, in your development section
you will be able to show your grasp of the economic facts of life during
Colbert's tenure of office and his rections to them. You then need a
strong conclusion in which you leave the reader in no doubt as to your
answer.

___

Source-based questions on Finance, Taxation and the Economy
1 The state of France
Read the royal proclamation about the Paris poor-house (page 53) and
Fénelon's letter to Louis XIV (page 67). Answer these questions.
a) How useful to the historian are these two documents as indicators of
    the social and economic condition of France in Louis XIV's reign? (6
    marks)
b) What do these documents tell us about their authors' attitudes to the
    poor and disadvantaged? (4 marks)
c) Do these documents suggest that their authors had constructive
    proposals for drastically improving the living and working conditions
    of poor people in France? Explain your answer. (5 marks)

CHAPTER 5

French Society in the Reign of Louis XIV

1 The Significance of Versailles

Eleven miles south-west of Paris stands Versailles, resplendent in its classical proportions, incomparable in its beautiful setting, vast in scale and conception. This famous palace is always seen as the physical representation *par excellence* of the Sun King's reign. And rightly so, for Versailles was planned and built in accordance with Louis XIV's wishes; a countryman at heart, he insisted on being surrounded by acres of carefully planned gardens and ponds, while the palace itself was all windows and balconies, a 'castle' in name only.

Louis imposed his conception on reluctant ministers and courtiers who preferred the convenience and bustle of Paris or the less pretentious palace at Marly. The grumpy duc de Saint-Simon loathed Versailles:

1 One might be for ever pointing out the monstrous defects of that huge and immensely costly palace, its orangery, kitchen gardens, kennels, larger and smaller stables, all vast, all prodigiously expensive. Indeed a whole city has sprung up where before was
5 only a poor tavern, a windmill and a little pasteboard chateau. That Versailles of Louis XIV, that masterpiece whereon countless sums of money were thrown away merely in alteration of ponds and thickets, was so ruinously costly, so monstrously ill-planned, that it was never finished. The avenues and plantations, all laid out
10 artificially, cannot mature and the coverts must continually be restocked with game.

Many have agreed with Saint-Simon. Versailles, it has been suggested, epitomised all that was wrong with French society between 1661 and 1715. Contemporaries and historians have depicted the Sun King surrounded by his courtiers indulging themselves while France starved. Or there is the familiar picture of Louis imprisoning his potentially creative nobles in an endless round of sterile court ritual. Or again, while the artistic excellence of the palace is conceded, we are told that this was an élite culture; 90 per cent of the population was left in unenlightened ignorance. This morally rotten edifice was hallowed by the Chuch, whose wealthy, absentee bishops scuttled round the corridors of Versailles, ignoring their dioceses to say nothing of the Bible's teaching on poverty. For above all Versailles allegedly represents the scandal of social and economic inequality, since the expense of financing the Sun King's and his courtiers' self-indulgence was met by the wretched tax-payer. And it was the poor who paid most.

However, much of this has been questioned by recent historians. Versailles may have been flashy and expensive; but it was not *that* expensive. It may have been built to the greater glory of Louis XIV; but this was all part of a rational, well-thought-out campaign with a recogniseable political purpose. Louis and his bishops, we are told, took their responsibilities seriously, as did the aristocracy; few of them were simply palace drones. Conditions in the towns and country may well have been far less adversely affected by Louis XIV's building programme than has been suggested, while the cultural impact of royal patronage of the arts was widespread and beneficial.

Above all we are reminded that the student of history must avoid anachronistic judgements. A twentieth-century democrat with socialist leanings may be repelled by the 'obscene' injustices of Louis XIV's France. But as L.P. Hartley reminded us in *The Go-between* 'the past is another country - they do things differently there'. Arguably Louis XIV would have had no idea what you were talking about if you had criticised the extravagance of Versailles. Our job as historians is to get inside the period, not to make moral judgements from outside it.

In this chapter you will have the opportunity to decide whether the old-fashioned, hostile portrayal of social conditions in the Sun King's reign is indeed oversimplified and misleading. Versailles acts both as a symbol and as a catalyst, breaking up easy generalisations, making us look again at the realities of the age, forcing us to use the evidence properly and empathise with seventeenth-century people; the mighty shadow of the palace broods over the whole of this chapter. At first sight Versailles does indeed symbolise the worst type of class society. On closer inspection it may have a different message.

2 The Estates

Louis XIV's France certainly was a class society. Everyone had his or her God-ordained place and woe betide those who tried to break the mould. For instance, peasants were punished for wearing gloves - a privilege of the nobility. There was a marked contrast with conditions across the Channel where, as one acute observer put it, 'riches make gentlemen in every country of England'. Ultimately great wealth might enable a Frenchman to become a nobleman; but it took time and persistence. France's extreme social conservatism took its cue from Louis XIV himself who was obsessed with order and rank.

Louis and his contemporaries thought in terms of 'estates' rather than 'classes'. The difference in terminology is significant. Our use of the word 'class' often goes with the recognition that social divisions are superficial, unjustifiable and subject to revision or abolition. The 'estates' of Bourbon France on the other hand were supposedly ordained by God and therefore permanent; they had a functional justification and were thus basically rational. There were three estates:

the clergy who prayed and preached, the nobility who defended the realm on the battlefield and the third estate which included everybody else. The third estate's subordination to their superiors was supposedly just in that all they did was make money through the law, manufacturing, trade or agriculture - ignoble and demeaning activities. However unreasonable these assumptions might seem today, that is the way seventeenth-century French people thought. The estates will therefore be our terms of reference in this chapter which seeks to explore the realities of society in Louis XIV's reign.

a) The First Estate: the Clergy

What had the first estate to say about the 'obscenity' of Versailles, about the gilded aristocrats who feasted there and the toiling masses who paid the bill? Whatever the message was, it was listened to with respect, for the seventeenth century was a religious age.

Virtually everyone believed in the existence of a spiritual world, which was influenced not only by God and his Church but also by the powers of darkness. There was certainly universal belief in the existence of the devil. Such superstition, as we might regard it, was by no means found solely among the ignorant. Mass in the royal chapel was allegedly not the only one celebrated at Versailles, for the king's mistress, Madame de Montespan, was accused of devil-worship and black masses. Gradually reason prevailed over superstition. Across the Channel, Lord Chief Justice Powell displayed the scepticism of an educated Englishman by acquitting a witch because there was no law against flying. French legal authorities were becoming similarly sceptical; there was concern over 'improper' use of torture and over the part played by spite in bringing charges against witches. Nevertheless, persecution of witches persisted in remote, backward areas such as Lorraine. Not only among illiterate peasants did the Bible remain a closed book, regarded as a source of magic incantations, only understood by the priest. Profound fear as well as profound love of God ensured that the first estate played a dominant role.

In such conditions the influence of the clergy on French society was bound to be considerable. Not surprisingly it was exercised emphatically in a socially conservative, conformist direction. This was partly due to the social structure of the Church. For while the majority of French clergy was bourgeois, the Church's leadership was aristocratic. This was a trend which was accentuated during the personal rule; while 61 per cent of bishops in 1661 were self-made careerists, this figure had fallen to 39 per cent in 1715. Louis XIV favoured real aristocrats, often from the unsophisticated south of France, who were less likely to ask awkward questions or adopt a critical approach to social issues. Compare the bourgeois Jacques-Benigne Bossuet, unquestionably the most eloquent and impressive ecclesiastic of his generation, who was rewarded with the remote Bishopric of Condom and then promoted to Meaux, almost in the suburbs of Paris - but that is where he stayed - and the aristocratic Louis-Antoine de Noailles whom Louis appointed Archbishop of Paris and who subsequently became a cardinal. *'Tout Noailles est imbecile'* was the popular verdict on the archbishop's brain-power, but there was no questioning his blue blood.

The first estate hallowed and buttressed the *status quo*. Men and women should cheerfully accept the place in society to which God had called them. They should look to the beyond, recognising that 'here we have no abiding city'. 'Fear God, honour the king and don't rock the boat' sums up the Church's social gospel, preached explicitly in sermons and implicitly in 'notices' at Mass which concerned such matters as the latest assessments of *taille*. Furthermore, the Church performed the state an immense favour by sweeping social injustice under the carpet by making itself responsible for poor relief. Much necessary and commendable work was done by the many religious charity organisations, especially in times of famine. Thus was the state relieved of the obligation to care for the poor. The secular authorities could concentrate on locking up vagrants, criminals and lunatics, while ignoring the problems posed by inequality and poverty.

The first estate enhanced the prestige of the Crown by approving the king's achievements. Every time a royal army was victorious, churches throughout France dutifully resounded to the *Te Deum,* the ancient hymn of praise to God. Furthermore, the clergy helped to finance the Crown's policies; although they did not pay tax, they voted the crown a substantial *don gratuit* - in theory a freely offered gift, in fact the product of tough negotiations. Even more valuable was the never-ending exhortation from pulpits up and down the land to honour the king. Bossuet was only the most celebrated of many preachers who taught that to resist royal authority was tantamount to blasphemy (see page 42 for Bossuet's approval of Louis' revocation of the Edict of Nantes). When the Jesuit Father Lombard, preaching at Versailles on the first Sunday in Lent 1703, told the courtiers and soldiers to honour God rather than the king, he created a sensation. Louis' confessor, Father La Chaise, who was also a Jesuit, apologised on behalf of his Order. To his credit Louis allowed Lombard to finish his course of sermons, but he was not invited to preach again.

In fact king-worship reached its apogee at Versailles. Here is a contemporary description of the courtiers at their devotions:

 1 The great persons of the nation assemble each day in a temple that
   they call a church. At the far end of this temple stands an altar
   consecrated to their God, where a priest celebrates the mysteries
   they call holy, sacred and fearful. The great ones form a huge circle
 5 at the foot of this altar and stand erect, their backs turned to the
   priest and the holy mysteries, their faces lifted towards their King

who is seen kneeling in a gallery, and on whom they seem to be concentrating all their hearts and spirits.

As for the clergy's message on everyday issues, the Church was in the grip of the Catholic reform movement, 'one of the greatest repressive enterprises in European History' (Briggs). This meant that important socio-political questions about the distribution of wealth were officially ignored in favour of more traditional preoccupations of the clergy. Certainly there was nothing progressive about the instruction parish priests passed on to their flocks. The confessional was used in order to inculcate guilt and fear, while the priest should keep a card-index of his parishioners' sins. Sexual relations were a special area where these moral absolutists laid down the law. Marriage was a regrettable necessity ordained by God to accommodate people who could not otherwise control their sexual urges. Even within marriage, however, the procreation of children was the only justification for sexual intercourse which on no account should be enjoyed.

The first estate disapproved not only of moral laxity but of the whole female sex. Women were assumed to lack both men's intelligence and their ability to control themselves. The only sure way for a man to avoid pollution was to shun female company altogether. 'Friendship with a wicked man is less dangerous than conversations with a godly woman' was typical advice for parish priests. Where women could not be avoided, the opportunities for sin had to be strictly limited. Women were censured for flaunting their breasts; Molière mocked clerical paranoia on this issue when his servant girl retorts 'You're mightily susceptible to temptation then!'. Village wakes and dances were discouraged as opportunities for young people to get together. Members of a family were not to sleep in one bed, in order to avoid incest. This last prohibition is a good example of the Church's lack of realism; there was no awareness that peasants slept together to keep warm and because they only had one bed - and indeed sleeping together might just as well discourage incest as promote it. Equally striking was the self-evident indifference towards female victims of sex-abuse within the home. Meanwhile, with male complacency, clergy attributed the pains of child-birth to Eve's sin in the garden of Eden.

On the other hand 'the great repression' certainly raised standards among the clergy themselves. There were very few absentee bishops at Versailles; the majority lived in their dioceses, founding seminaries for the training of priests, conducting visitations and insisting on overall decency and efficiency. Indeed, parish priests could hardly criticise their parishioners if their own lives were scandalous. An episcopal visitation of the diocese of Rouen in 1698 condemned 43 curés for drunkenness and sexual misconduct; given that there were approximately 3,000 priests in the diocese, this was a remarkably small figure which compared well with standards prevailing a century before. There was widespread satisfaction when Harlay the Archbishop of Paris died of apoplexy without receiving the sacraments - clearly divine judgement on his irregular private life; there could be no such criticism of his successor, Cardinal Noailles. The French Church of the seventeenth century produced its saints such as François de Sales whose guidance on sexual issues, incidentally, was sensible and humane.

Meanwhile realism tempered dogma as clergy grappled with overcrowding and crime in urban shanty-towns and with superstition and ignorance in the countryside. The ideals of the moral absolutists were often unattainable. Village wakes survived, as did traditional cults of local saints which the reformers condemned as superstitious. The fact that 10 per cent of brides were pregnant when they got married suggests that the campaigners for sexual apartheid achieved incomplete success.

Nevertheless, the contribution of the first estate to the stability of Louis XIV's France was considerable. The clergy co-operated with the Crown in producing a conformist, conservative, Catholic society. Nothing illustrates their success better than the almost universal approval for the persecution of the Huguenots (see pages 42). This was a triumph of persistent propaganda over common sense and, we might think, Christian charity. But it is an excellent example of Louis XIV's policy of using religion to integrate society; the Catholic clergy were his willing accomplices and the majority of the French people readily accepted the message. Religion was indeed the opiate of the masses; or perhaps 'social cement' might be a better description.

Would it then be anachronistic to expect the first estate to have been more critical of Versailles and all that it stood for? Probably. However, it is thought-provoking that *some* clerical protests were voiced. Towards the end of the reign Fenelon, the Archbishop of Cambrai, attacked the king's disregard for his people. Bossuet called Versailles 'the city of the rich'. Significantly a number of radical *curés* embraced Jansenism (see pages 46) which asked questions about social justice and stood for more demanding standards than those adopted by the Jesuits who dominated the royal establishment. The wealth of the senior clergy and the selfishness of the nobility were pilloried in sermons and pamphlets which circulated in Paris. But not at Versailles; all that was in evidence there was the enthusiastic support which the first estate and the mighty edifice of royal absolutism gave each other with unquestioning consistency.

b) The Second Estate: the Nobles

Did Versailles witness the emasculation of the French nobility? Are we to accept the picture which Saint-Simon has so memorably painted of blue-blooded aristocrats enmeshed in court ritual, trapped like flies in amber, while middle-class administrators ran the country? The taming of the nobility was indeed one of Louis XIV's indisputable achievements (see pages 26-7). And it is true that with the single exception of Beauvilliers all Louis' ministers were members of the new nobility who had made their name as administrators rather than as soldiers. There certainly was a spectacular increase in the numbers and influence of the nobility of the robe (as they were called) during Louis XIV's reign - a process intensely resented by the ancient nobility of the sword. But was this the whole story?

In fact Saint-Simon oversimplified a complex situation. For one thing the nobles who held the king's shirt at his morning *lévèr* or accompanied him to Marly were but a fraction of the nation's ancient aristocracy. The court only settled at Versailles in 1682; before that date there would have been no room for droves of aristocrats as the king moved around his various houses. Even after the move to Versailles only 4,000 members of the nobility at most could be accommodated in the excruciatingly cramped quarters provided for them in the great palace; but there were about 100,000 aristocrats in France as a whole.

Certainly life at Versailles involved the nobility in endless ceremony and ritual, all of it designed to emphasise the majesty of the Sun-King. Louis XIV lived and died in public. When he got up (his *lévèr*) he was surrounded by courtiers; it was a privilege to witness the king dressing. He would have breakfast in public, relieve himself in public, go to Mass in public, have lunch in public, go for a walk in the afternoon or hunt in public, have dinner - the main meal of the day - in public, play billiards or cards in public and finally go to bed in public. At this, the king's *coucher,* it was a privilege to hold a candle while the king got into bed. Were there any royal activities which were *not* public events? Clearly the king conferred with his advisers off stage. But Louis had to build country retreats so that he could escape public gaze to enjoy sex with his mistresses.

This never-ending public ritual involved Louis and his nobles in stringent rules of etiquette. It was an offence to turn your back on even a *portrait* of Louis XIV and it was customary to take your hat off in the presence of the king's dining table whether he was there or not. Historians discuss the extent to which Louis introduced more formality than there had been in previous reigns; possibly his Spanish blood to say nothing of his Spanish wife encouraged rituals formerly seen in Madrid but not in Paris. Louis himself was an expert on court pageantry, but the greatest authority became Monsieur, Louis' brother. The aristocracy had to conform to the petty tyranny of these Bourbon sticklers for etiquette. Louis resembles a queen bee perpetually surrounded by his drones, the obsequious blue-blooded aristocrats.

But were they merely drones? In fact, involvement at court was only one of the nobility of the sword's activities, for Louis XIV welcomed their co-operation in the highest echelons of church and state. Provincial governors were invariably noblemen. In a less exalted but nevertheless important role we find relatively obscure aristocrats such as François de

Castellane, comte de Grignan, who led the nobles of Provence in war, halting Eugene's invasion of France in 1707. Indeed, military and naval commanders were almost invariably noblemen while even the most assiduous courtiers followed their traditional *métier* on the battlefield. In time of war Versailles resembled a military hospital full of men in bandages and on crutches. Or again, we have noted the increasing proportion of aristocratic bishops during the reign. In the diplomatic service while mere noblemen of the robe went as ambassadors to republics such as the United Provinces or Venice, noblemen of the sword monopolised the embassies at the courts of Louis' fellow monarchs - London, Madrid, Vienna. So it is nonsense to suggest that the French nobility were given no responsibility.

Indeed it would be strange if it were otherwise, for in Louis XIV blue-blooded snobs like Saint-Simon had their greatest ally. Louis believed profoundly in the importance of rank, order and deference. He enjoyed the company of men of birth, playing cards or billiards with them, safe in the knowledge that they would not presume on his condescension. The last thing which he wanted to do was to undermine the prestige of the nobility or blur class distinctions.

However, Louis did indeed incur Saint-Simon's wrath by reinforcing a trend which went back to Henri IV's time; as we have seen, a new aristocracy, the nobility of the robe, had been created and was now substantially increased. Although it was socially subordinate to the nobility of the sword, it exercised influence in government. The sword nobles looked askance at this process, objecting to the very idea that these *parvenus* (upstarts) should be considered nobles at all.

Why then if he was such a snob did Louis XIV encourage this growth of the nobility of the robe, which was such a marked feature of his reign? Why did he treat them with such respect, vetoing for instance Colbert's wish to abolish the *paulette* (see page 29)? For two reasons: he needed the robe nobility's services and he needed their money. Louis preferred his ministers to be noblemen of the robe; because they were not members of long-established families, they were dependent on his favour - his 'creatures'. Furthermore, during the personal rule, both central and local government became more bureaucratic. Ministers and secretaries of state created their own administrative back-up, while in the localities *intendants* recruited *subdélegés* - assistants who unlike the *intendants* came from the local office-holding aristocracy. Where were these administrators to be found but in the *parlements* and in the urban municipalities? Service of the Crown brought ennoblement. However, Louis XIV ennobled far more members of the wealthy bourgeoisie than he needed for royal administration. These new-rich social climbers paid for the posts which the Controller-General dreamt up, so desperate was the Crown for money. So Louis' expensive foreign policy explains the rise of the robe nobility.

However, the nobility of the sword were determined to keep their distance from these recent additions to the nobility. And very successful they were, simply because the qualifications to belong to the old nobility were well known: ancestry which could be traced back to the fourteenth century, a record of service to the crown on the battlefield and the behaviour and life-style of a genuine aristocrat. This could be expensive, and there was always available the oldest solution to an aristocrat's extravagance - to marry money. However, such *mésalliances* did not happen very often; they pained the king and although Colbert's daughters married dukes, Louis once paid a blue-blooded courtier's debts to save his family from such disgrace.

It was indeed a great life for the nobles, both of the sword and of the robe. Both at court and in their localities they dominated the social scene, basking in the envy of their inferiors. For the most part they were rich enough. The sword nobility monopolised the best jobs in Church and State apart from the royal bureaucracy, where the robe nobility came into its own. Despite the rule that they were not allowed to involve themselves in trade, the nobles were well integrated into the complex spoils system of tax-collection. Not only were they exempt from the payment of tax; many of them actually made fortunes out of the exploitation of the poor who had to pay the taxes.

Versailles fairly represents the domination of France by the second estate. There was the fount of patronage where nobles had to come in order to receive jobs, lands, money. Not to be known at court could be fatal; 'we never see him', was Louis' sentence of social death on any nobleman who had failed to register his presence - and like many drawing-room martinettes Louis missed nothing. From Versailles too went out the orders for the governing of France and her empire. Contrary to what you might suppose from the traditional picture, the recipients of these orders were as likely to be noblemen of the sword as of the robe. But robe or sword, they were still members of the second estate, the chief beneficiaries of Versailles.

c) The Third Estate

Versailles, the 'city of the rich', was built by the poor. Even after the court had moved there in 1682, there were 22,000 workmen toiling in the buildings and gardens. The cost in terms of human life was notoriously high. Madame de Sévigné wrote 'of the great mortality affecting the workmen of whom every night wagons full of the dead are carried out as though from the Hotel-Dieu; these melancholy processions are kept secret as far as possible in order not to alarm the other workmen'. Louvois ruined the king's Swiss guards by putting them to work on digging a lake in the palace gardens, while thousands of soldiers died in the abortive attempt to divert the river Eure across an aquaduct to feed the royal fountains.

Members of the third estate not only built Versailles, they also paid for it. In his biography of Louis XIV François Bluche argues that Louis' expenditure on his buildings was not excessive. In an extravagant year, 1683, these accounted for only 2.35 per cent of national expenditure; from 1661 to 1715 Versailles 'cost no more than 68 million livres'. 'Looked at objectively', Bluche continued, 'these are not astronomically high figures'. This may be so. However, the point is that this expense was not met by the clergy and the nobles who lived in luxury at Versailles, but by the rest of French society. Furthermore, within the third estate those who were richest paid least.

Life indeed could be comfortable for capable or lucky members of the bourgeoisie. Some were even successful in climbing socially, basing their ambitions on solid economic achievement. Vast bourgeois fortunes were made in industry and commerce, for instance in the great trading communities of Marseille and Lyon. The particular trend of the reign was enrichment in government service, especially tax collection.

One of the reasons why the bourgeoisie wished to climb socially was the unattractiveness of the town; how much pleasanter to lead the life of a country gentleman! Overcrowding, bad sanitation and polluted water made the towns very unhealthy; cholera, typhoid and plague were common. Overcrowding occurred because it was prudent to live within the medieval walls; not only were frontier districts vulnerable to enemy invasion but supposedly friendly armies were definitely not welcome. Violence flourished within the walls despite the efforts of urban militias. Here are a typical town-dweller's comments:

1 What do I or any of his subjects care if the prince is happy and
   showered with glory through his own actions and those of his
   followers, or if my country is powerful and feared, while I, anxious
   and miserable, lead a life of oppression and poverty; if, protected
5 from enemy attacks, I find myself perpetually threatened by the
   assassin's dagger in the streets and squares of the city, so that I am
   afraid of being robbed not so much in dense forests as at the corner
   of my own street; if town life lacks the security, order and
   cleanliness which would make it pleasant, and which would bring
10 calm and prosperity to the community?

In truth the real beneficiaries of town life were Louis XIV and the local oligarchs. The towns were subject to increasing royal domination. The *intendants* supervised the elections of mayors and members of town councils. They interfered with municipal finance, often with good reason, as towns were inclined to get into debt and thus would not be able to pay tax. In Paris Louis XIV insisted on the police force being revitalised; in 1667 he appointed La Reynie as Lieutenant of Police, charged with the maintenance not only of law and order, but also of the city's hygiene, street-lighting and censorship; by 1715 the capital had 5,522 street-lights. This exceptionally close involvement by the Crown can be explained by Louis' touchiness about the capital's potential for trouble-making. In general, royal policy contented itself with the control of town oligarchies to the mutual profit of king and favoured members of the bourgeoisie.

For there were definitely winners and losers. Not all town-dwellers were upwardly mobile. In fact the majority were imprisoned in a fixed social and economic environment. Most urban economies were static rather than dynamic, parasitic rather than creative; trade and manufacture were stifled by tolls and regulations and were dependent on the local peasant farming communities which were often as not themselves in deep recession. Urban communities were usually dominated by judges and other royal officials; the way to preferment was to join them, because you certainly could not beat them. The majority of town-dwellers could do neither, for repressive municipalities and guilds made it impossible for artisans to set up business on their own; they were regimented and exploited without any prospect of self-improvement. For instance, the silk-workers of Lyon were fined if they missed a day's work, took too much time off for meals, took their tools home, used bad language at work or failed to observe instructions. At St Maur des Fosses near Paris workers had to begin the day by standing by their looms, making the sign of the cross and offering their work to God - on pain of dismissal.

If the squalor of urban life was a far cry from Versailles, in the rural communities the contrasts between rich and poor were even more marked. As Louis XIV's reign progressed the richer peasants who owned their land and possessed equipment and animals distanced themselves from their less fortunate neighbours. The ever-increasing demands of the taxmen drove the less capable peasants into debt. Furthermore, the government's tax-agents tended to conspire with the richer peasants at the expense of the poorer; as the historian Pierre Goubert remarks, 'there was nothing democratic about a French village'.

Nevertheless, one should not exaggerate the wretchedness of life for the peasants in Louis XIV's reign; or at least one should be cautious about generalising. The village community looked after its own. It was a closely knit society in which strangers were shunned, eccentrics were persecuted as witches and every now and again the government's tax-collectors were beaten up. The vast majority of peasants lived and died within sound of the bells of the parish church in which they were christened. The community enjoyed its festivals, its wakes, and its ritual fights with the next village.

The English poet and essayist Joseph Addison has left us this vivid picture of the French people in 1700:

1 I never thought there had been in the world such an excessive magnificence or poverty as I have met with in both together. One

can scarce conceive the pomp that appears in every thing about the
King, but at the same time it makes his subjects go bare-foot. The
5 people are however the happiest in the world and enjoy from the
benefit of their climate and natural constitution such a perpetual
mirth and easiness of temper as even liberty and plenty cannot
bestow on those of other nations ... there is nothing to be met with
in the country but mirth and poverty. Everyone sings, laughs and
10 starves.

However, there were times when it was not possible to laugh and sing.
Indeed, occasionally peasant communities protested violently. In 1675
the peasants of Lower Brittany revolted against their overlords and
against royal tax-collectors. Their leaders produced a charter called the
Peasant Code which is a revealing document:

1 1. The right to demand a share of the harvest and to require labour
services, as claimed by the nobles, shall be abolished.
2. The hearth-tax shall be used to buy tobacco, which shall be
distributed with the consecrated bread at parish masses, for the
5 gratification of the parishioners.
3. Vicars and priests shall be paid a fixed salary for their services to
their parishioners, and shall not be able to claim the right to any kind
of tithe, or to demand any additional payments for all their other
religious duties.
10 4. Justice shall be administered by able men chosen from among our
honourable citizens, who shall be paid a salary... stamped paper shall
be held in execration by them, so that even the memory of stamped
paper shall be entirely blotted out.
7. Hunting shall be forbidden to everyone, whosoever he be from the
15 first day of March until mid-September, and dovecots shall be burned
down and permission given to kill pigeons in the fields.
8. It shall be permissible to go to the mills when one chooses and
millers shall be compelled to give back flour of the same weight as the
corn.
20 (Signed) The Skull-breaker and the People.

The circumstances which produced this remarkable manifesto were
exceptional. The Dutch War (1672-9) seriously damaged Brittany's
trade as well as causing unprecedentedly high taxation. Furthermore,
Brittany was not a typical province in that it had only been part of France
since the fifteenth century. When the revolt was suppressed one observer
heard peasants shouting 'mea culpa' - 'the only French they knew',
('Mea culpa' is Latin for 'it's my fault').
Nevertheless, we know from other sources that the grievances which
the Skull-breaker listed were highly typical of French rural society as a
whole: resentment at the arrogance and greed of the nobles whose

hunting ruined the crops and whose marauding pigeons the peasants were not allowed to kill, hatred of the taxes on salt and of new taxes such as the one recently introduced on paper for legal documents, reluctance to pay the priest more than was reasonable, and distrust of millers who were proverbially on the fiddle. Ruthless threats against people who would not co-operate indicate how desperate the leaders of the revolt were; and sure enough they were soon to be hanged after the government had liaised with the local aristocracy and suppressed the revolt with troops. Justice was by no means administered 'by able men chosen among our honourable citizens' then or at any other time.

Versailles might have been a million miles away; the Sun King inhabited another world, remote from the concerns of the third estate. Once when a merchant was received at the palace, Louis XIV had no idea how to behave to him. As for the peasantry, when Monsieur brought their sufferings to the king's attention, Louis replied: 'Do not trouble yourself, brother, about such matters. If four or five thousand of such *canaille* were to die, would France be diminished?'

3 The Arts

The artistic and intellectual achievement of the reign which Versailles epitomises did not simply happen; it was planned, with definite objectives in mind. The king and his assistants deliberately executed a cultural campaign to which the great palace was the climax. We have seen that Versailles was the king's home, the focus of the court and the centre of government. It was also the showpiece of French artistic and cultural exuberance. This flowering of the French creative spirit was hardly a natural growth; to a great extent it was forced, with the purpose not only of glorifying France, but also putting across a flattering image of Louis XIV's style of kingship. This is the message which Versailles conveys, throwing significant light on the link between French politics, society and the arts.

Many historians have implicitly recognised the existence of this cultural campaign. However, in his *The Fabrication of Louis XIV* (1992) Peter Burke has explicitly analysed this manipulation of the media. He has shown how artists, architects, musicians, writers were methodically recruited to glorify France, personified by Louis XIV.

In the early years of the reign Colbert masterminded this cultural offensive. When Louis put him in charge, he said to Colbert 'I confide to you what is the most precious thing in the world which is my glory'. The king himself was a discerning patron, well aware how important a role the arts can play in boosting a régime's image. But it was Colbert who provided the dynamic vision. As Superintendent of Buildings he adopted the same masterful and interventionist role with regard to the arts as he brought to the direction of the economy. Indeed, Colbert never lost sight of economic priorities; the celebrated Hall of Mirrors at

Versailles was an advertisement for French glass, while the tapestries which depicted Louis' triumphs were made at the royal Gobelins works, subsidised by the government.

Typically Colbert's solution was to regiment French artists, sculptors and architects by requiring them all to join the *Academie Royale de Peinture et de Sculpture* (1663). This was followed by the Academies of Science (1666), Architecture (1671), Music (1672), and the *Comedie Française* which was established in 1680 to encourage French drama. Colbert was advised by an inner cabinet of aesthetes and intellectuals such as Charles Perrault, the author incidentally of *Little Red Riding Hood,* and the artist Charles le Brun who both dispensed the Academies' patronage to other artists and produced influential paintings himself.

Colbert believed that Paris was the ideal location for magnifying the king's glory. He directed the rebuilding of the Louvre, the royal palace in the centre of Paris, recruiting the internationally famous Italian architect Bernini. However, Louis not only vetoed Bernini's plans but also Colbert's proposals for further expenditure on the Louvre. He already had his eyes on Versailles; Bernini was sent home, the only memento of his visit to France a bust of the young king (see page 86).

Burke argues that Colbert's death in 1683 marked a watershed in the campaign to 'market' or 'fabricate' Louis XIV's image. He was succeeded by Louvois who adopted a more aggressive style. For instance, 20 enormous equestrian statues of the king were erected in major cities, in theory in response to spontaneous public enthusiasm, in fact on the instruction of M. de Louvois. A statue of Louis in the Place des Victoires in Paris bore the inscription 'To the Immortal Man' which many religious people considered blasphemous. Again, collections of medals were mass-produced and circulated, offering a brash summary of the history of the reign - for instance, 'Twenty towns in Flanders captured by the Dauphin', 'Two million Calvinists converted'. Above all, Louvois supervised the never-ending development of Versailles, the centre of the cult of the Sun King. Once Louvois mobilised hundreds of foresters so that a wood which Louis disliked could literally collapse before his very eyes - a trick copied centuries later by Martin Bormann to gratify Hitler.

For two decades Versailles had already played a significant role in the presentation of Louis' image. Louis had fallen in love with the place when it was only an unpretentious hunting-lodge built by his father in a peaceful forest. In the perfect early summer of May 1664 he staged a pageant for the court, *The Pleasures of the Enchanted Isle,* theoretically in honour of the queen though everyone realised that Louis' mistress Louise de la Vallière was the real enchantress. The king himself took part in a theatrical cavalcade. Lully the court musician presided over the music while Molière wrote *Tartuffe* for the occasion. Louis enjoyed this send-up of religious hypocrisy, although both his mother and his wife were outraged. The point of such aristocratic fun and games should not be missed: the play was a publicity exercise, full of compliments to the Sun King.

When Louis decided to turn Versailles into the finest palace in the world, he first employed the trio who had made Fouquet's Vaux-le-Vicomte so offensively beautiful: Le Vau the architect, Le Brun the painter and Le Nôtre the gardener. Together they created the impressive ensemble of gardens, lakes, statues and buildings which delight today's tourists. Everything conforms to a perfect design. Once when Madane de Maintenon complained about the cold, Louis replied 'Well, at least we shall all die symetrically'.

The whole palace advertises Louis XIV. Everywhere Louis is compared to Apollo the sun-god. Louis also appears as Jupiter the king of the gods and Neptune the god of the sea. Le Brun's influence is in evidence, especially his preference for order and decorum; he rejected a birth of Christ which included humble cattle. His own *Crossing of the Rhine in the Presence of the Enemy* which can be seen in the Hall of Mirrors is typical; it is an impressive, pompous piece of propaganda, showing the French army's victory over the Dutch in 1672, with Louis and his generals dressed as Roman heroes. The classical prejudices of the Academy come across more attractively in Charles de Lafosse's *Jason Landing at Colchi* on the ceiling of the Salon of Diana; the artist has been allowed to produce a much livelier study of real people.

Louis XIV himself insisted on being consulted before his artists put their ideas into practice. For example he turned down Le Brun's first proposals for the Hall of Mirrors, insisting that he himself was to appear in the paintings rather than heroes of antiquity, and that the captions emphasising the triumphs of the reign were to be in French and not Latin, so that everyone could understand them. Louis also inspired the decorations surrounding the staircase of the ambassadors which commemorated his triumphs over Spain, Holland and the Empire. Visiting ambassadors ascending this staircase to be received by the king no doubt felt suitably overawed as they mounted the steps.

Everywhere were portraits of the king; Louis must have spent a significant part of his life sitting for his artists. Sometimes a particular event is recorded. For example there is a painting of the Doge of Genoa apologising to Louis XIV for building ships for the Spanish navy; he had come to Versailles to grovel. Burke has pointed out that Louis' publicity men even mastered the technique of 'the media event', that is to say, an event which never happened; there is Testelin's splendid portrait of Louis presiding over the Acadamy of Sciences which he never visited (see opposite page). Such portraits show Louis in the prime of life, gorgeously dressed, arrogantly self-confident. It is worth comparing them with Rigaud's portrait (1700) (see front cover); though the face is an old man's, care-worn and wracked with pain, the stance is still masterful. Thackeray's witty parody of Rigaud is only partly true (see page 86), for he misses the skill of the royal portrait painters; more than

Louis XIV at the Academy of Sciences by Testelin

Bust of Louis XIV by Bernini

You see at once, that majesty is made out of the wig, the high-heeled shoes, and cloak . . . Thus do barbers and cobblers make the gods that we worship.

Cartoon by William Thackeray

barbers and cobblers were needed to package the Sun-King.

The worries of Louis' old age were made bearable by his court musicians, for Versailles was also the venue for the development of French music. Jean-Baptiste Lully was a versatile composer, director and colleague of Molière in the production of court ballets and masques in which Louis himself took part. Lully made a fortune out of court music by cleverly excluding his rivals. Louis XIV adored Lully's work which, despite being a little insipid, still retains its charm. The king was a keen amateur musician himself, playing the lute and the guitar and singing enthusiastically in a rather tuneless way. After Lully's death he himself interviewed candidates for the post of chapel organist. Visitors came from afar to hear the king's choir.

Versailles also attracted writers who were glad to sing the Sun King's praises. We have noted Molière's role in return for which Louis protected him against the disapproval of the *dévots* - one of his most enlightened actions. Racine who wrote tragedy of a similar quality to Molière's comedy was another court propagandist. 'I would have praised you more if you had praised me less', Louis once remarked to Racine. Nevertheless, he took him on campaign as his official historian. The quality of this state-sponsored literature is a matter of opinion. Louis once asked Racine who was the greatest writer of the reign. 'Molière' said Racine. 'Really?' replied the king 'You surprise me, but then you know more about such matters'. Certainly Molière still reads well, even in translation. Similarly notable were the achievements of the Academy of Science; among many scholars of repute Colbert recruited the Dutchman Huygens who developed the telescope and the pendulum clock. Louis himself in theory joined in literary pursuits by producing elegant and supremely complacent memoirs to instruct the Dauphin; but they were largely ghosted.

The Dauphin was also subjected to propaganda from the king's favourite thinker, Jacques-Benigne Bossuet, the eloquent Bishop of Meaux. It has been unkindly remarked that never was such formidable erudition wasted on such an unpromising pupil, although it has been suggested that the Dauphin was not as stupid as he looked. However, it is to be doubted whether he made much of Bossuet's presentation of history in which Moses dwarfed modern French philosophers such as Descartes, Augustine corrected the dangerous biblical criticisms of Richard Simon and the ancient Romans beckoned the Dauphin to imitate them on the battlefield; not that they could compare with Louis XIV who 'being equal in valour to the most famous ancients surpasses them in piety, wisdom and justice'. The proof of Louis' piety was his eradication of heresy.

However, rather inconveniently, the age produced livelier minds than Bossuet's. For Louis XIV could not destroy freedom of thought which was sweeping through Europe. Even in the theological sphere, disturbing ideas circulated (see page 46); Bossuet demanded the suppression not only of Simon's brilliantly unorthodox biblical criticism but also of Jansenist and Quietist writings. Indeed, censorship was imposed to an increasing extent towards the end of the reign. Under the influence of the Jesuits Louis banned the works of Descartes. But he could not suppress the Protestant writings of the exiled anti-monarchist Jurieu or the rationalist sceptic Bayle, nor could he prevent Huygens resigning from the Academy of Science as a protest against French atrocities in his native land. Scurrilous rhymes attacking the king and Madame de Maintenon defied the censor, while in measured and rather self-satisfied prose Fenelon told the king that he should be ashamed of himself. While this criticism was a reaction to Versailles rather than its product, the palace gave birth to a critic of genius, the duc de Saint-Simon; historians question his reliability but they all quote him. Meanwhile by the end of the reign Voltaire and Montesquieu were looking on the world with amused scepticism; Louis was by now completely out of touch with modern ideas, an embarrassment and an incumbrance to France's livelier minds.

However, Louis XIV's image-makers adapted to changing circumstances. He reacted to criticisms of his lust for military glory and sexual gratification by modelling himself on his holy ancestor, Saint Louis. In 1689 the king ostentatiously melted down the famous Versailles silver dinner service to buy bread for his starving people. And it is again as the father of his people that Louis appealed to the French public for one last effort in 1709, in Torcy's eloquent prose.

This shift of emphasis was reflected in the changing face of the great palace. When it became Louis XIV's home in 1682, his mistress the marquise de Montespan had to be accommodated. She was provided with a gorgeous suite of rooms at the top of the grand staircase plus an annexe on the ground floor beneath the king's appartments, - the celebrated bathroom suite. And what a bathroom! The walls were decorated with paintings by Le Brun, sculptures and marble columns, while the bath was cut from a single piece of marble costing 15,000 livres. Twenty years later the scene had changed. The final addition to the palace was Mansart's sober chapel, built in stone not marble, containing a shrine dedicated to Saint Louis. Montespan had been banished long ago. Now the king's favoured companion was his prudish wife, Madame de Maintenon, their chief preoccupation no longer the gratification of his body but the salvation of his soul.

Not all the cultural achievements of the reign came from Versailles. Apart from the subversive and critical literature which we have noted, artists such as Claude Lorrain and Watteau painted spontaneously and with compassion such topics as scenes from peasant life. Not surprisingly these artists were ignored by the royal image-makers. However, what is particularly impressive is the sophistication and effectiveness of the government-inspired Versailles media industry. A considerable number of talented artists, musicians and writers offered a carefully packaged presentation of royal absolutism. By its artistic qualities Versailles made France king-worshipping and conformist.

4 Conclusion: All Done With Mirrors?

There is a strong case for arguing that Versailles helped to widen the divisions in French society during Louis XIV's reign. By isolating the king, his ministers and his courtiers from the nation, Versailles significantly contributed to this process. It is indeed both illustration and cause of increasing social and economic inequality.

However, the traditional picture of the first two estates living a life of pointless futility at Versailles has to be revised. The nobles were far more involved in the real world than used to be appreciated, sharing real power and real profits with the king and his ministers. Meanwhile, the clergy encouraged the less privileged members of society to accept meekly the gross inequalities which Versailles represented and the dominant role of the king and of the first two estates.

Perhaps the chief contribution of Versailles to the social stability of the reign was propaganda. For the *image* of sacred, centralised absolutism which emanated from Versailles was partly based on fact, but partly on media-manipulation. There was a real element here not only of clever presentation but also of pretence. It is significant how Louis himself was obsessed with *appearances*, with creating the right impression. Once he caught a cold in the head because he dithered for half an hour deciding which wig to wear. Or again when he welcomed his grandson's child-wife Marie-Adelaide of Savoy, he was worried that she curtseyed badly. In a letter to Madame de Maintenon he reiterates, 'We shall *have* to do something about that curtsey'.

Louis set the tone for Versailles. Its artificiality comes across in recorded conversations: 'What time is it?' 'Whatever time Your Majesty wishes it to be'. 'When does your wife expect her baby to be born?' 'Whenever Your Majesty says'. 'I'm afraid you're getting wet.' 'Sire, the rain is never wet at Marly'. To this day Versailles is impressive. But was not its whole culture a pretentious veneer, a game of make-believe at which Louis himself excelled but which others could not always maintain, or indeed did not wish to maintain?

For instance Louis XIV may have had exquisite manners, but even his own relations did not always copy him. Saint-Simon gives a vivid description of Louis' cousin the duc de Vendôme. This aristocratic *roué*, instantly recognisable by the cover over his syphilis-ravaged nose, would dictate orders and receive visitors while seated on his *chaise-percée* (portable lavatory). 'He evacuated copiously and the pot was carried away in front of the entire company. On the days when he shaved, the same pot was used'. It was as though Vendôme was acting out an uncouth parody of Louis' XIV's court ritual. Lest it be thought that this was simply the free-and-easy way in which soldiers behaved in camp, compare this Versailles conversation-piece as described by Louis XIV's sister-in-law, Monsieur's second wife Liselotte:

1 One evening the four of us were alone here in this drawing-room after supper, namely Monsieur, myself, my son, and my daughter. After a long silence, Monsieur, who did not consider us good enough company to talk to us, made a great loud fart, turned
5 towards me, and said, 'What is that, Madame?' I turned my behind toward him, let out one of the selfsame tone, and said,'That's what it is, Monsieur'. My son said, 'If that's all it is, I can do as well as Monsieur and Madame', and he also let go of a good one. With that all of us began to laugh and went out of the room.

Now, as we saw in the first chapter, Louis' brother, his sister-in-law and his nephew had every reason to despise the Sun King and his facade of civilised behaviour. Do we have here an understandable contempt for the pretentiousness of Versailles, Louis XIV and his court?

If the apparent refinement of court life was a facade, this makes the success of the Versailles public relations campaign all the more remarkable. Thackeray suggested that Louis XIV was invented by his barber and his cobbler. However, we have established in this chapter that there was more to the fabrication of the Sun King and of Versailles society than that. What is very striking is that so few of Louis' contemporaries saw through the trick.

Peter Burke argues that the fabrication of Louis XIV was aimed at three audiences: the French, foreigners and posterity - including us. Perhaps the campaign had least impact on the Third Estate. Louis' media offensive did little to offset his unpopularity with the poor towards the end of his reign. Although anyone could admire the statues and triumphal arches prominently displayed for Louis' glory, nevertheless most of the artistic and literary achievements of the reign did indeed constitute an élite culture. Parish registers reveal that 70 per cent of people getting married could not sign their names; so they would be unaffected by the literary products of the Versailles intelligentsia. An even higher proportion would never have the opportunity of listening to Lully's music or enjoying Molière's plays.

So which sectors of French society was Louis trying to impress? Undoubtedly, the people who mattered. In theory anyone could visit Versailles and admire the court if they were properly dressed and could afford to hire a sword. In practice this meant the nobility of the robe. Louis was happy for such people to admire him from afar provided they did not damage his gardens. However, the real audience at whom the reign's cultural offensive was targeted was the aristocracy. By their imitation of the Sun King the nobles showed how much they admired him, how effective the media-campaign was.

The Sun King's reputation abroad is remarkable. Louis XIV's

propaganda was meant to inculcate both fear and admiration. Many European rulers came to fear French aggression more than the facts warranted. For to a certain extent the deliberately created threat of unstoppable French absolutism was a myth. In the event the very success of the French media rebounded so that Louis found himself confronted by formidable coalitions which were too much for him. *Nec pluribus impar* (not unequal to more) proved to be untrue. But French propagandists wanted France to be admired as well as feared. Here Louis XIV's media hype led to slavish imitation. Copies of Versailles sprang up all over Europe, notably in Vienna, St. Petersburg and Madrid. The Earl of Montagu was just one of many English country-gentlemen who built a mini-Versailles. French fashions, French manners, French styles of painting, French literature were the rage. Although millions of Frenchmen still spoke their own local patois, French became the language of diplomacy and of society all over the world.

And what about posterity? Louis XIV and his media specialists certainly aimed to impress future generations. The foundations of their buildings contained medals sunk into the masonry, with the intention that they should be discovered centuries later. The palace of the Sun King was built to last. Louis' fame and even his notoriety are tributes to the success of the fabrication campaign. To this day even the most critical historians concede that Louis XIV was 'a great king'. As for Versailles, where was Bismarck's Reich to be proclaimed but in the Hall of Mirrors (January 1871) and where was the treaty to be signed which terminated that empire but in the same incomparable setting (May 1919)? Witness also the popularity of Versailles today as a tourist attraction. Louis would be sardonically gratified by the hoardes of Americans, Japanese and other nationalities who tramp round Versailles today, equipped with cameras rather than swords. When I last visited the great palace, it had obviously not lost its magic, even if those famous mirrors needed cleaning!

Today the corridors of the great palace no longer echo to Lully's music, the clink of billiard balls or the sound of hushed laughter as men lost their fortunes or women their virtue. Nevertheless, Versailles still eloquently represents both an ideal and an evasion. The ideal was a conservative Catholic society dominated by an absolute monarchy. It was by no means an absurd or an ignoble ideal. However, Louis XIV's version of this ideal involved an evasion, a deliberate turning away from the imperfections of French society. Instead of trying to effect changes or improvements, Louis and his ministers chose rather to glorify, glamorise and misrepresent the status quo.

Versailles is not the only example in history of the concealment of unpalatable truth beneath a gorgeous facade. All pageantry fulfils this function. The state opening of parliament, an elaborate cathedral service, the ritual of the law courts, the flummery of founder's day at a great school - all these proclaim both idealism and a defensive urge to conceal secretly-admitted defects. But no-one could swing it like the Sun King. That is the message of Versailles.

Making notes on *French Society in the Reign of Louis XIV*

You are least likely to be set exam questions on the contents of this chapter: an occasional essay on social conditions, perhaps a question on the role of the nobility, conceivably something on the arts, with particular reference to Versailles. But only one such question would be found over the years compared to ten, say, on Louis' foreign policy or on the revocation of the Edict of Nantes.

Whether therefore you need to work your way through this chapter, noting everything, is doubtful. Perhaps the best tactics would be to read it through rapidly, (so that you are aware of its contents and can use it as a 'quarry' for details and ideas on other exam topics), and merely to note down a few headings that will later serve to remind you of the main points. An essay on Louis XIV's religious policy for instance would be enriched by the material in this chapter on the social role of the first estate.

However, this is not to suggest that this chapter is unimportant. Far from it. You may be well advised to make a thorough note on the inequality and unfairness of the age. If you do this, keep Versailles in view, making a 'running' summary of its role and significance. In particular you should home in on Louis XIV's use of propaganda. You might even be set questions based on Peter Burke's *Fabrication of Louis XIV;* be prepared.

Source-based questions on *French Society in the Reign of Louis XIV*

1 Louis XIV's Portraits

Carefully study the portraits of Louis XIV by Rigaud (front cover) and Testelin (page 85), the bust by Bernini (page 86) and the cartoon by Thackeray (page 86). Answer the following questions.

a) What do these sources tell you about the changes which took place during Louis XIV's life to his health, his personality and character? (6 marks)

b) Do you agree with Thackeray's implicit suggestion that Louis XIV's real characteristics were concealed by court painters and sculptors? Explain your answer. (6 marks)

c) In what ways can portraits be used as evidence by historians? (3 marks)

2 Life in the French Countryside

Carefully read Addison's description of rural France (page 80) and the skull-breaker's manifesto (page 81). Answer the following questions.

a) Based on what you know of living conditions in France during Louis XIV's reign, how far does Addison's description surprise you? (4 marks)

b) Explain the skull-breaker's references to i) taxes on paper, ii) the right to kill pigeons, iii) hunting across peasants' fields and iv) the powers of the clergy. (8 marks)

c) Explain i) the context of the publication of the skull-breaker's manifesto and ii) the motives of those who wrote it. (8 marks)

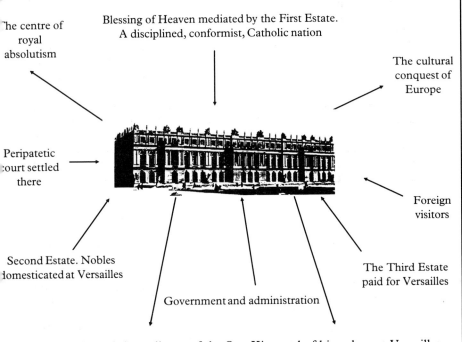

The centre of royal absolutism

Blessing of Heaven mediated by the First Estate. A disciplined, conformist, Catholic nation

The cultural conquest of Europe

Peripatetic court settled there

Second Estate. Nobles domesticated at Versailles

Government and administration

Foreign visitors

The Third Estate paid for Versailles

The magnetism and the radiance of the Sun King and of his palace at Versailles

Summary: French Society in the Reign of Louis XIV

CHAPTER 6

Louis XIV and Foreign Affairs - the Early Years, 1661-84

1 Attitudes and Objectives

Louis XIV's foreign policy has always been a contentious topic. His critics have compared him with Hitler, alleging the same unlimited ambitions, the same willingness to risk war, the same indifference to human suffering, the same eventual futility. However, the Sun King has had his defenders too. Both François Bluche and Ragnhild Hatton have maintained that Louis' foreign policy was conceived in France's true interests, that Louis should be credited with genuine achievements and that his contemporaries were more ready to go to war than he was. In the following two chapters the evidence will be presented, including contemporary accounts and judgements, and the present writer's views will be expressed. But the reader must decide where the truth lies.

In this first section we shall explore Louis XIV's attitudes to foreign policy and discuss what he was trying to achieve. Were the principles on which he acted and the aims of his foreign policy worthy of our respect or of our contempt? Caution is essential. Not only are there the problems of bias and hindsight. The trap must also be avoided of generalising too readily about the events of a very long reign. Louis' point of view was unlikely to be the same in 1715 as it had been in 1661. At the same time this does not rule out the possibility of consistent priorities doggedly pursued.

One fundamental attitude Louis XIV certainly adhered to throughout his reign. He was convinced that he was fully qualified to conduct France's foreign policy in person. He thought that because foreign policy was essentially a royal preserve, God had equipped him with the necessary qualities in order to succeed; in his memoirs he boasts of his innate common sense and self-control. Louis supplemented these divinely-bequeathed gifts with a thoroughly professional approach, for he was hard-working and extremely well-informed. He was kept up to the mark by his world-wide diplomatic service and by experienced advisers at home. Louis therefore felt that he was justified in dominating France's foreign policy; it was appropriate that he himself should take the decisions and determine the priorities.

What were those priorities? Bias has certainly influenced the answers which historians have given to this question. Louis' admirers have credited him with greater perspicacity and consistency than he in fact possessed and his enemies have accused him of ambitions which he never held. For example, it has been claimed that Louis XIV was a far-sighted statesman, aiming at the pacification of Europe in the general interest, though in reality he tended to be more selfish. On the other hand the accusation that he sought universal domination was a myth circulated by his enemies. Likewise Louis' alleged campaign to establish a universal religion is a figment of Protestant propaganda.

Perhaps the most damaging allegation is that the Sun King was excessively concerned with *la gloire*. Certainly Louis was obsessed by the military prowess of his father and grandfather and of the victories which had been achieved during their reigns. Sometimes a legitimate and understandable ambition to make his mark in European politics and maintain the family tradition degenerated into a wish to show off and achieve cheap triumphs at other people's expense. This was especially the case in the earlier part of his reign. Sometimes Louis thought too much in dynastic terms and not enough about the welfare of people affected by his policies. But the Sun King was neither a monster nor an irresponsible adventurer. Although he was capable of acting selfishly, he took his role as 'the Most Christian King' seriously, accepting obligations both to God and to his people.

These obligations did not necessarily conflict with *la gloire*. For we need to understand that for Louis and his contemporaries *gloire* meant much more than the acquisition of a military reputation. *Gloire* meant professional integrity and loyalty to principles. Thus Louis would never countenance assassination as a weapon to employ against his enemies; such a fall from grace would be against his *gloire*. In the same way the surrender of land which was essential for the defence of France would diminish Louis' *gloire*. If therefore it is accepted that Louis consistently pursued his *gloire*, we need to remember that the term involved not simply acquiring a reputation as a warrior but truly and idealistically fulfilling his *raison d'être* as a king.

Louis' pursuit of *gloire* certainly involved him in the Spanish succession. The possibility was always there that Louis himself or a member of his family might obtain the prize of Spain and her empire, for in June 1660 Louis XIV had married Maria Theresa, the daughter of Philip IV of Spain. In September 1665 Louis' father-in-law, Philip IV, died leaving the throne to his infant son Carlos II. This pathetic weakling - he was a syphilitic paralytic - was not expected to live for very long. The monarchs of Europe eagerly awaited Carlos the Sufferer's death - not least Louis XIV as he was married to Carlos's older sister and was determined to make the most of his wife's claims. No-one could have predicted that Carlos's sad life would last until November 1700. At times Louis seemed to have lost patience with his sickly brother-in-law who refused to die, and to have shelved the matter of the ultimate fate of Spain's huge empire in favour of short-term land-grabbing. Nevertheless, this great issue was always there as a priority and can never have been far from Louis XIV's mind.

Nor did France's national security ever cease to be a priority. To a great extent Louis' foreign policy was dictated by the diplomatic events of 1648. The Treaty of Munster, which concluded the Thirty Years

War, had been Mazarin's masterpiece. France had received the best possible concessions that could be wrung from the Habsburgs (the Emperor and the King of Spain), who had temporarily been frustrated in their attempts to dominate Europe and humiliate France. However, a number of issues had deliberately been left unresolved because neither side had been willing to concede defeat. Notably the fate of Alsace had been left far from clear. The Emperor had ceded the province to the King of France, but clause 89 had excluded Strasbourg, the capital. Similarly French ownership of Metz, Toul and Verdun had been reluctantly conceded by the Habsburgs, but the fate of Lorraine which these three fortresses controlled had been left unsettled. No King of France could sleep easily while such issues were undecided, for a vulnerable and weakly defended eastern frontier invited the nation's enemies to invade, as they had so often done in the past.

Similarly recent events had demonstrated the vulnerability of France's north-eastern frontier. In 1636 a Spanish army had invaded from the Low Countries and had only been stopped at Corbie, in the virtual suburbs of Paris. During the *Frondes* revolts France had been invaded from the same quarter by traitors with Spanish assistance. The frontier between France and the Spanish Netherlands bequeathed to Louis by his predecessors was unsatisfactory - untidy, illogical and hard to defend. In the distance there beckoned the Rhine, but it was improbable that a king of France would be allowed to push his frontier so far to the north. In practical terms there were no natural boundaries such as mountains or sizeable rivers, and the existing frontier was full of militarily non-viable indentations and projections. Here was indeed a challenge which Louis could not ignore. As we have seen, *gloire* included maintaining national security. If necessary blood must be shed and treasure expended for this goal.

Whether Louis XIV was too fond of war, as he is supposed to have admitted on his deathbed, is another matter. A discussion of this supreme question is best postponed to the conclusion of our chapters on Louis' foreign policy. Suffice it now to establish that the Sun King had his principles, nor were his ambitions unreasonable. Furthermore, his was a troubled inheritance: a vulnerable country surrounded by jealous enemies in an unstable Europe.

2 Ways and Means, 1661-7

What chance had Louis XIV of achieving his aims when his personal rule began? To answer this question we must examine France's strengths and weaknesses compared to those of her neighbours. And we must establish with what success Louis XIV prepared France for the struggles in which she would be involved if his aims were to be achieved.

Europe in 1661 was both unstable and exhausted. The Peace of the Pyrenees (1659) between France and Spain had brought to an end almost half a century of dynastic warfare which had involved virtually the whole of Europe apart from the British Isles. This gigantic conflict between the Habsburg powers of Spain and the Holy Roman Empire on the one hand and Bourbon France and her allies on the other had brought devastation and misery to millions. Germany in particular had been systematically ruined. Even countries such as France, whose territory had been almost untouched by fighting, were weakened by the expense of the wars. The whole of the seventeenth century was a period of recession, falling prices and declining populations in Europe. Although such generalisations are risky due to the uneven nature both of natural disasters and military devastation, it is perhaps valid to claim that this general economic malaise had been exacerbated by the wars. What can be said with complete safety is that at the beginning of Louis XIV's personal rule there was a power vacuum in much of Europe brought about by general impoverishment and weariness.

However, France was less exhausted than her neighbours and was well-placed to exploit this power vacuum. Her young, clever, dynamic ruler personified the country's potential authority and influence. The land of France was a fertile source of government revenue. The diplomacy and military initiatives of Richelieu and Mazarin had won for France a position of great strength *vis-à-vis* the other European powers. Louis XIV had chosen as his motto the Latin words *Nec Pluribus Impar* which literally mean 'not unequal to more'; a better translation would be 'I can take on the whole world'. In 1661 it looked an appropriate motto.

Not that the Sun King's resources were in perfect condition when he began his personal rule. Far from it. While the army was being reorganised and re-equipped, Richelieu's navy had virtually disintegrated. The diplomatic corp was demoralised by Mazarin's death. Above all, the treasury on which everything depended was in serious debt. However, the speed and efficiency with which Louis XIV transformed this gloomy situation was remarkable.

Under the king's direction Colbert restored the royal finances, while Le Tellier and his son Louvois transformed the administration of the army. A war department, responsible to the secretary of state, supervised military regulations, salaries and pensions, intelligence, troop movements and reinforcements. An important innovation was the army magazine, a food supply centre for troop concentrations which eliminated the unpopular billeting of troops on civilians. Gradually the purchase of commissions was diminished in favour of selection on merit so that one of Louis' greatest soldiers, Vauban, was able to become a marshal of France without once buying promotion.

Further reforms followed. Martinet, the Inspector-General of Infantry, introduced marching in step and became a byword for discipline. *Esprit de corps* improved among the infantry regiments who now wore uniform and vied with each other in healthy rivalry on the battlefield. Separate artillery, specialised engineers and marines made their appearance. Vauban displayed his mastery of the science of fortification and invented the modern bayonet, enabling the French soldier to fire his musket and stab his opponent simultaneously. Colbert established arsenals for the manufacture of cannon. When Louis created 37 new cavalry regiments in December 1665, the administrative support was on hand - and indeed for the even more spectacular expansion of the army later in the reign.

The king himself was intensely interested in all these developments. He was never happier than when reviewing troops or campaigning. Perhaps he seldom breakfasted in no-man's land, as William of Orange did before the Battle of the Boyne while cannon-balls decapitated his staff-officers, but Louis did command in the field and there is no truth in the charge that he was a coward. The fact is that, unlike William of Orange, he had plenty of able commanders and that the most valuable service he could give his armies was behind the lines, co-ordinating and administering. This was Louis' role during the first six years of his reign and he performed it very well.

Another myth is that Louis XIV was not interested in the navy. While he was a soldier by inclination and training, he was too intelligent not to be aware of the importance of sea-power. In 1662 he gladly purchased Dunkirk from the King of England for 5,000,000 francs, appreciating its value as a naval base. In 1665 he made Colbert responsible for naval affairs and supported him consistently. As a result, the French navy increased from nine ships of the line in 1660 to 112 by 1683. When vessels of all types are included the French total by that date was 220, 45 more than the Royal Navy. Naval arsenals were developed at Brest, Toulon and Rochefort, maintaining a formidable naval presence both in the Atlantic and in the Mediterranean. French technicians developed the bomb-ketch, a sophisticated shell which was much more advanced than any comparable projectile fired from Dutch or English ships. A tradition of French seamanship was established, enabling Louis XIV's ships to give a good account of themselves both against the English and the Dutch.

Meanwhile Louis XIV took a firm grip on French diplomacy, supporting his representatives with a combination of threat and bribery. Soon German princes and bishops, the Kings of England, Hungary and Poland and Swedish noblemen were on France's pay-roll. Meanwhile the Royal Navy had to salute the French flag, the Spanish ambassador had to give way to his French colleague in London and the Pope had to apologise after a fracas between his Corsican and the French ambassador's guards. It was apparent that the Most Christian King meant business.

Indeed, with the co-operation of the wise and experienced secretary of state for foreign affairs, Hugh de Lionne, Louis XIV soon achieved even more solid diplomatic successes. In 1662 a commercial and defensive treaty was signed with the United Provinces. Charles II of

England was persuaded to marry a Portuguese princess, and as Portugal was France's ally, this was reflected the fact that England was now firmly in the Sun King's orbit. Military initiatives backed up the diplomats. The Dutch were supported against the Bishop of Munster and French troops helped to save Vienna from the Turks in 1664.

3 The War of Devolution, 1667-8

The *status quo* in Europe was drastically altered by the death in 1665 of Philip IV of Spain. As we have seen, he was succeeded by his infant and unhealthy son, Carlos, with Philip's widow acting as regent. Louis XIV believed that this temporary weakness of the Spanish government could be exploited to France's advantage. The vulnerable north-eastern frontier could be strenghthened, either by extracting concessions from Madrid through diplomacy or by war.

Louis therefore decided to advance his wife's claims to the Spanish inheritance. French lawyers produced an ingenious argument for taking part of the Spanish Netherlands. There was an ancient Flemish law that when a man married a second time his property should eventually 'devolve' upon the children of his first marriage. Maria Theresa was the child of Philip IV's first wife, Carlos of his second. Maria Theresa was therefore the rightful heir to territory in that part of the world. This argument was in fact threadbare as the law of devolution applied only to private property, and the Spanish Queen Regent rejected the French case. This prompted Louis to recall an even older adage - that possession is nine points of the law. So he prepared to invade what he claimed as his wife's property.

The manifesto sent by Louis XIV to the Spanish court reveals the light in which he wished his aggression to be seen:

1 It is not either the ambition of possessing new states or the desire of winning glory by arms which inspires the Most Christian King with the design of maintaining the rights of the queen his wife; but would it not be shame for a king to allow all the privileges of blood
5 and of law to be violated in the persons of himself, his wife and his son? As king, he feels himself obliged to prevent this injustice; as master, to oppose the usurpation; and, as father, to preserve the patrimony of his son. He has no desire to employ force to open the gates, but he wishes to enter as a beneficent sun by the rays of his
10 love, and to scatter everywhere in country, towns and private houses the gentle influence of abundance and peace which follows in his train ... Heaven not having ordained any tribunal on earth at which the kings of France can demand justice, the Most Christian King has only his own arms to look to for it.

To say the least, Louis was economical with the truth. His manifesto was propaganda though by no means untypical of the time. Louis did in fact relish the opportunity to demonstrate the excellence of his recently reformed army and to direct its operations.

For months the French military machine had been demonstrating its readiness for war. At a parade in May 1666 the household cavalry and the French and Swiss guards saluted the king and queen, the four-year-old Dauphin marching at the head of his regiment to his parents' delight. This was the first of many displays culminating in a magnificent review at Amiens a year later when the royal party included not only the king and queen but de la Vallière, the mistress on her way out, and de Montespan, the rising star - a bizarre company indeed. But there was nothing bizarre about the army of 50,000 men which Louis now threw into the disputed lands.

Castel-Rodrigo, the governor of the Spanish Low Countries, with only 20,000 troops could not prevent the French from helping themselves to numerous important and valuable towns, notably Douai, Charleroi, Oudenaarde and Lille. Turenne was in operational command, while Vauban conducted the sieges. Louis was in his element, at one moment showing off to his wife and mistresses, at the next sleeping rough with the troops. He looked weather-beaten and thinner but the demands of army life did not stop him trimming his moustache for half an hour every morning before a mirror.

France's successes continued, demonstrating the excellence of her army and the readiness of Louis XIV to use it. England and the United Provinces were sufficiently impressed to conclude a war which they had been fighting and persuaded Sweden to join them in a triple alliance. This was signed at the Hague in January 1668 and was designed to limit Louis XIV's gains. Louis retaliated by opening negotiations with the Emperor Leopold for the eventual partition of the Spanish empire. Before these negotiations bore fruit, Louis dispatched Condé to conquer Franche-Comté - in mid-winter. Condé was Louvois' choice, at the expense of Turennne who had become increasingly insubordinate towards the 'civilians' conducting the war. ('One would not send such orders to the stupidist man in the kingdom!' he had complained about one of Louvois' interfering missives). Condé seized his opportunity and Franche-Comté was overrun by mid-February.

Louis now displayed moderation. He supported the doves (Lionne, Colbert and Le Tellier) against the hawks (Louvois, Turenne and Condé) when the Spaniards were prepared to talk. By the treaty concluded at Aix-la-Chapelle in May 1668 France agreed to restore Franche-Comté to Spain on condition that she could keep many of her conquests in the Spanish Low Countries. Vauban was now able to go ahead with the creation of a complex network of fortresses, including Armentières, Oudenaarde and Lille. Ironically most of these acquisitions were in Walloon Flanders where the laws of devolution did not apply.

So ended the first of Louis XIV's wars. It was relatively uncostly in human lives, a classic example of the lightning war which Louis always hoped to fight. But, although the capacity for destruction of seventeenth-century warfare was as nothing compared to modern times, inevitable suffering was caused to people living in the cities stormed by Turenne and in Franche Comté when it was overrun by Condé. However, there is no indication that Louis was aware of this. The 'Most Christian Mars', as contemporaries called him, had enjoyed his first taste of blood. In his memoirs Louis comes across as supremely complacent; he was proud of his armies' success and of his own moderation as the victor. It was indeed the case that strategically valuable additions had been made to France's north-eastern frontier.

Louis XIV was also in a great rage. The object of his wrath was human ingratitude. The guilty men were the Dutch. Oblivious of the fact that France had protected them in the past, they had had the effrontery to combine with the Swedes and the English against their benefactor. They even lampooned Louis in humorous rhymes, to say nothing of excluding French merchandise with protective tariffs. Louis' determination to teach the 'the maggots' a lesson was perhaps the most important result of the war.

4 The Dutch War, 1672-9

While there is a case for the War of Devolution which resulted in improved French security, it is harder to justify the Dutch War. With patent vindictiveness between 1668 and 1672 Louis openly prepared for the invasion of Holland, while his ministers stifled whatever reservations they may have felt about the rightness of this course.

Not that the Sun King wanted a long and expensive war. On the contrary this was to be another lightning strike, meticulously planned, brilliantly conducted and purposefully concluded. The Dutch were to be taught a lesson so that they would never again interfere with the Sun King's absorption of the Spanish Netherlands. It is unlikely that Louis hoped to conquer a great deal of the Dutchmen's land; it would be sufficient to wrap their knuckles sharply for their ingratitude and insolence. If in addition their trade could be ruined, this would please Colbert who had become a late convert to war against the Dutch.

Louis took the necessary steps to isolate the United Provinces. Lionne bribed the Swedes to withdraw from the Triple Alliance. He then negotiated a treaty with Charles II the details of which were finalised by Monsieur's wife, Minette, who was Charles's sister. The details of this agreement, which was signed in May 1670 at Dover, pleased Louis exceedingly. In return for French cash Charles promised to declare himself a Catholic and to join France in war against the Protestant Dutch. In a memorandum to Lionne Louis happily referred to 'continuation of contacts with England to attack and ruin the Dutch'.

Preparations for the coming war included the re-occupation of

Lorraine in order to limit potential enemy access to the Low Countries and to protect France's eastern frontier. Meanwhile, the final touches were added to the mobilisation of the French army. The Dutch, justifiably worried, sent their ambassador to offer whatever concessions were necessary. Madame de Sevigné described what happened.

1 Yesterday the Dutch ambassador presented his letter to the King who did not look at it although the Dutchman offered to read it. He pointed out that the States General had never acted other than in a polite way, yet this great army was prepared for the sole
5 purpose of attacking them. The King then spoke in a wonderfully majestic and gracious manner, said that he was aware that they were stirring up his enemies against him and that he considered it wise not to allow himself to be taken by surprise. He was powerful on land and sea in order to defend himself. He would do whatever
10 he considered was necessary for his *gloire* and for the good of the state. He then nodded to the ambassador in such a way as to indicate he did not want any reply.

On 6 April 1672 France declared war on the United Provinces. By mid-June Louis' soldiers had captured 40 Dutch towns and the Dutch had abandoned their barrier fortresses. Amsterdam was there for the taking if Louis had accepted Condé's advice to dispatch the cavalry. But he listened to the more cautious counsel of Louvois and Turenne and the chance was missed. Future events would show just how serious Louis' mistake was. However, in the heady atmosphere of summer 1672 it looked as if the king's dreams were to be fulfilled. On 22 June Jan de Witt, the Dutch leader who had always been in favour of friendly relations with France, sent envoys to discuss surrender terms. The Dutch offered to pay an indemnity and to concede to France all Dutch territory south of the river Maas.

Louis XIV rejected the Dutch offers, since Louvois was sure that even greater concessions could be extracted. So the fighting continued. As a result of this prolongation of the war several things happened. First, the Emperor Leopold and the Elector of Brandenburg moved their armies to the Dutch Republic's assistance. 'I am in for a long war', Louis remarked. Secondly the Dutch checked the invaders by opening their dykes and flooding the countryside. Thirdly, an Amsterdam mob lynched Jan and Cornelius de Witt, thus bringing William of Orange to power as stadtholder - an office reserved for the Orange dynasty in times of crisis. To Louis' amazement William assumed the leadership of his country's resistance. He was to devote the rest of his life to the salvation of Holland and the frustration of Louis XIV.

Here was another fine example of Dutch ingratitude! Louis had frequently intervened in William's interests. Louis had even invited William to marry one of his illegitimate daughters, provoking the retort that 'my family has been accustomed to marry the daughters of kings, not their bastards.' Louis persistently underestimated William of Orange. Puny physique, wretched health and a forbidding personality concealed a good mind and a great heart. Ironically, as a young man William had had a touching admiration for France and her splendid monarch. But events were to prove to Louis' cost that William could also be a great hater.

He certainly was not a great general. Although the war had now escalated to a degree far beyond Louis' intentions, for the next five years French troops had no difficulty in winning victories. Despite the formation of an anti-French alliance in 1673 involving the Empire, Brandenburg, Spain and Lorraine, Louis could write in his memoirs: 'I therefore ended that year not reproaching myself for anything and not believing that I had lost a single occasion to assure and extend the limits of my kingdom'. And indeed yet more towns fell to French assault in the Low Countries. Franche-Comté was overrun again. Turenne won spectacular victories against the imperialists, before being killed by a stray cannon-ball in July 1675. While peace negotiations were in process in the winter of 1678, Louis XIV himself hurried matters along by a fast-moving campaign to capture Ghent.

Meanwhile, the navy acquitted itself creditably. The Dutch were experienced and well-equipped at sea so that initially Colbert's pride and joy found the going tough. In the battle of Sole Bay (1672) a joint Anglo-French fleet was mauled by the Dutch under de Ruyter. But the French achieved their revenge four years later when they defeated the Dutch at Agosta in the Mediterranean; de Ruyter died of his wounds. Meanwhile, in the Atlantic French privateers harassed Dutch trade.

Nevertheless, the desirability of peace was now apparent to all, including Louis XIV. After entering the war without enthusiasm, England pulled out in 1674 and was now allied to Holland through the marriage of Charles II's niece Mary to William of Orange. Sweden which had joined the war on Louis' side had been defeated by the Elector of Brandenburg at Fehrbellin (1675). Above all, the French economy was strained by the war. The French army had swollen to 280,000 but, despite its size and its professionalism, stalemate had resulted. It was proving difficult to find successors to Turenne and to Condé who had retired mortified by Louvois' interference. It was time to settle.

As a result of the prolonged negotiations at Nymegen (summer 1678), France retained Franche-Comté and towns in Flanders, such as Saint-Omer, Aire, Ypres, Cambrai, Bouchain and Valenciènnes. Freiburg strengthened France's eastern frontier. On the other hand, Louis handed back to the Dutch his most northerly conquests. In February 1679 two further treaties were signed at Nymegen - between the Emperor and Sweden and between the Emperor and France. Louis offered to hand Lorraine over to its duke - who was a prince of the empire - but on such humiliating terms that the duke preferred to remain an exile, leaving the French in occupation of his duchy.

So ended the Dutch war. Louis was dissatisfied with his gains, subsequently sacking Pomponne for not achieving better terms. However, others were impressed. The Elector of Brandenburg wrote, 'In the present state of affairs it seems that no prince will henceforth find security and advantage except in the friendship and alliance of the King of France'. It was perhaps significant that negotiations at Nymegen were conducted in French and not Latin, hitherto the accepted language of diplomacy. A few months later the city of Paris bestowed on Louis XIV the title 'Great'.

Yet Louis' unease was even more justified than he appreciated. He was certainly aware of the alarm that his victories had created. Indeed, in his memoirs he attributes the anti-French coalition of 1673 to the fact that his armies had been too successful. 'The advantages that my armies had just gained over the United Provinces having surpassed everyone's expectations had at the same time excited the hatred and jealousy of my neighbours.' But it is doubtful if Louis appreciated the extent to which France was now hated and distrusted.

For Louis XIV's version of French imperialism had provoked a force still more dangerous than the Emperor Leopold and William of Orange. By committing atrocities in Holland and the Palatinate French troops had behaved badly by the standards of the age, provoking widespread criticism. Louis consistently failed to appreciate the importance of public opinion, regarding foreign affairs from a largely dynastic point of view. Events would prove him wrong.

There were even more radical grounds for Louis' dissatisfaction. While French gains were real enough, did they justify the war? Given the widespread hostility towards France which the war had provoked, had the decision to attack the Dutch been a mistake? Did Louis XIV have to attack Holland? Louis's biographer, François Bluche, calls the Dutch war 'the inevitable conflict', basing his argument on the irremovable opposition of the United Provinces to French expansion in the Spanish Netherlands. Bluche also stresses the economic rivalry between Holland and France as well as the deep-rooted antipathy between Catholic and Protestant. The reader must decide whether these arguments justify the description of the war as 'inevitable'.

In fact, Louis might have achieved his aims by continuing the policies of his predecessors which had served French interests well. That is to say, under the cardinals France had allied with the Dutch and with the German princes in order to strengthen France's diplomatic and strategic position in Europe. By attacking the Dutch in 1672 and by prolonging the war, Louis turned his back on his predecessors' policies. Louis' change of course would have made more sense if he had persisted with Pomponne's alliance with the Emperor, which had produced the partition treaty of 1668. But by alienating Leopold as well, Louis provoked a truly cosmopolitan anti-French coalition which boded badly for France's future. The short-term gains of the Dutch war did not compensate for the long-term damage to France's international position.

Furthermore, even Louis recognised that, given his desire to annex Spanish territory, he was fighting the wrong war against the wrong enemy. In a revealing memorandum of October 1671 he referred to 'efforts to keep the Spanish from joining the Dutch and then to make them join'. In other words the Dutch were first to be humiliated and next the Spanish were to be encouraged to join them so that they too could be robbed of the territory which France needed. In which case, why make war on the Dutch at all? The decision to attack them was clearly emotional, not rational. After the Dutch had been punished, the real goal would still be the conquest of the Spanish Netherlands. If that was indeed the chief French priority, then Louis' correct long-term policy was to reassure the Dutch, not to humiliate them.

Even so, if Louis had acted with restraint after Nymegen he could have lived down the hatred and suspicion which he had caused. He was now to demonstrate that success can be harder to handle than misfortune.

5 From Nymegen to Ratisbon, 1679-84

If France was economically embarrassed by the Dutch war, so too were her enemies. Although William of Orange wanted to go on fighting, no-one would follow him. Charles II of England was happy to become a French pensioner again, while the Elector of Brandenberg now realised that it was wiser to ally with the King of France than to oppose him. As for the Emperor Leopold, he was both exhausted by the war and distracted by the Turkish threat. So in the immediate aftermath of the peace of Nymegen there was a power vacuum even more favourable to France than the one at the beginning of Louis XIV's personal rule.

Louis had every intention of exploiting this situation to the full. While his enemies with relief disbanded their armies, Louis maintained his at 140,000 men. The threat of force combined with bribery and enterprising diplomacy would work wonders. The enterprising diplomat was at hand. In November 1679 the king dismissed Pomponne, his secretary of state for foreign affairs: 'I have suffered for many years from his weakness, his obstinacy, his laziness, and his incompetence. He has cost me dearly and I have not profited from all the advantages that I could have had. I must finally order him to withdraw'. Louis replaced Pomponne with Colbert de Croissy.

This was a significant appointment. Colbert de Croissy was an experienced jurist who knew the Treaty of Munster backwards. He knew France's eastern frontiers equally well, having been the *intendant* in Alsace and president of the *parlement* of Metz. He had been ambassador to the Nymegen peace conference which, he was well aware, had by no means removed the obscurities of the 1648 settlement. These Colbert de Croissy was determined to exploit on his royal master's behalf.

Courts were now established known as *Chambres de Réunion* - at Tournai for Flanders, Besancon for Franche Comté, Metz for the bishoprics of Metz, Toul and Verdun, and Breisach for Alsace. The purpose of these courts was to investigate French claims to the ownership of territory which in the middle ages had been 'dependent' on towns now occupied by France. Colbert de Croissy discovered various such 'dependencies' which were now submitted to the *Chambres de Réunion*. These courts invariably found for the King of France, and their judgements were supported by artillery if necessary.

This policy of 'reunions' was doubly significant. First, the territory acquired was considerable: Montbeliard, the county of Chiny, and towns in the Saar and in Lower Alsace. Secondly, the identity of the powers who were victimised marked a new departure, for hitherto Louis had seized land from France's traditional enemies, the Habsburgs, or from the Dutch who, he was convinced, had become his enemies. But now he robbed his friends - the German princes who had always looked to France as their protector, or the King of Sweden whose duchy of Zweibrucken the court at Metz declared to be 'dependent' on France.

Protestations against Louis' exploitation of these long-forgotten customs were unavailing. Louis was seemingly unimpressed when Charles XI of Sweden indignantly broke off diplomatic relations. When the Duke of Wurtemburg and the Elector of Trier in their turn appealed to the imperial Diet against Louis' reunions, the French ambassador explained disingenuously that his master was enforcing the terms of the Treaties of Munster and Nymegen and that Louis' purposes were purely defensive. This may indeed have been the case, but it was little consolation to those who had been robbed when Vauban arrived to construct 'defensive' fortifications. He aimed to establish the *pré carré*, as France's north eastern frontier came to be known (literally 'square meadow' which meant a duelling-field; 'buffer zone' best conveys the meaning). Louis XIV and Louvois were perpetually on the move, inspecting Vauban's latest masterpieces, designed to make the reunions permanent.

In September 1681 French expansion provoked even more widespread alarm. Louis XIV, Louvois and 30,000 troops seized Strasburg. This was a free city of the empire to which France could lay no claim whatsoever. Louis gratified Catholic opinion by insisting that Protestant worship in the cathedral should cease. A magnificent *Te Deum* greeted Louis' triumphant entry into the city; he rode in a golden coach pulled by eight horses. Simultaneously French forces occupied the vital fortress of Casale in Northern Italy. Yet more 'defensive' work for Vauban!

France's north-east frontier at Louis XIV's death

French aggression continued at the expense of the Habsburgs. The king's tribunal at Metz had put forward claims which the King of Spain had refused to recognise. The governor of the Spanish Netherlands was therefore informed that a French army would be billeted in his provinces. Louvois supervised this operation, including the demand for a ransom of three million livres. Spain's ally Genoa was bombarded by a French fleet and burned to the ground. In October 1683 Carlos II declared war, but there was little he could do to frustrate French plans. Similarly helpless was the Emperor Leopold as he was involved in a life and death struggle with Hungarian rebels and invading Turks. He won a great victory at Kahlenberg in September 1683 which saved Vienna, but it took him five more years to pacify his eastern lands. Louis virtuously boasted of his idealism in not attacking the Emperor's lands in 1683. But in June 1684 he made the most of the Emperor's distractions by seizing Luxembourg. The King of France's enemies understandably called him 'the Most Christian Turk'.

At the truce of Ratisbon in August 1684 Spain and the Empire recognised Louis XIV's latest conquests. The reunions were accepted as permanent, while France was to retain Strasbourg, and Luxembourg for the next twenty years, during which time a truce would prevail. The construction of a magnificent fortress at Strasburg indicated that Louis intended his conquest to be permanent. This was Vauban's masterpiece, built with materials floated down the Rhine so that the fortress could be completed before anyone could object. French public opinion was delighted that the peace of Nymegen had been 'rectified'.

It was also a great time for French expansion overseas (see the map on page 61). This was spear-headed by missionary activity, notably by French Jesuits in Cochin-China and Siam. In West Africa explorers opened up the hinterland between French Senegal and Niger. The slave trade flourished between France's African colonies and her West Indian possessions such as Santo Domingo and Martinique. French explorers led by Cavelier de la Salle followed the Mississipi to the sea; they called it the river Colbert after their patron and the new colony Louisiana after their king. In the far north French colonists were challenged by the more numerous English; Louis XIV retaliated by appointing a governor for the whole of northern Canada.

Contemporaries were impressed by the style of French expansion, by the magnificence of French embassies including fireworks displays with the sun as their motif, by French literature often extolling the Sun King, by French art and architecture, above all on display at Versailles. Opinions might differ about 'Louis le Grand', but it was certainly *la grande siècle*. The worldwide stampede to imitate everything French, to speak French and to visit France unquestionably indicated the most profound admiration and respect.

Louis XIV is often said to have reached the height of his achievement at the truce of Ratisbon. It is certainly fascinating to guess the exalted place in history which he would have held if he had died in late 1684. Given his remarkable successes in war and diplomacy which were reflected also in France's cultural leadership of the civilised world, would anyone have begrudged him the title 'great'?

How do we account for Louis XIV's achievements between 1661 and 1684? They were undoubtedly due to a combination of France's strength and her rivals' weakness. French resources may at times have been strained, but in 1684 at any rate showed no signs of collapse. Indeed, by 1688 the army had expanded to 300,000, while the naval arsenals at Toulon and Brest had reached new heights of sophisticated efficiency. Louis' diplomacy continued to be backed up by apparently inexhaustible bribery. Louis' enemies on the other hand had always been a motley collection, often in total disarray. The fact was that the Dutch burghers disliked war more than they feared France so long as French policy was reasonably circumspect. Louis learnt from his mistakes so that in the mid-1680s William of Orange failed to galvanise his countrymen into action precisely because Louis XIV was careful to respect Dutch susceptibilities. The Emperor Leopold only gradually emerged as a significant rival to Louis XIV; as we have seen he had other, more pressing problems. The German princes were proverbially selfish and unreliable; well handled, or rather, well bought, they would always betray their allies. As for England, her foreign policy was erratic and her armed forces negligible until William of Orange transformed the situation in the 1690s.

Much of the credit for France's impressive showing belongs to Louis himself. It was not simply that there was a power vacuum enormously in France's favour. Louis XIV made the most of the international situation and skilfully utilised the advantages of the unified command which he exercised in contrast to the chaotic confusion of his enemies. He intelligently exploited France's geographical position as well. Her enemies never knew where the next blow would fall; Louis' assaults on Ghent in 1678 and Strasbourg in 1681 are good examples of this.

However, there were flaws in Louis XIV's achievements. First, the apparent strength of the French position in 1684 was deceptive. Ragnhild Hatton has argued that Louis was rightly worried by the intentions of the Emperor Leopold: 'Louis at the time was convinced, and so were some of his advisers, that once Leopold had achieved peace with the Turks on his terms, he would turn against France'. Furthermore, Hatton stresses the incomplete nature of Louis' campaign to strengthen France's security, especially on the persistently vulnerable north-eastern frontier. Despite Vauban's efforts the lack of a natural barrier inevitably made a permanently satisfactory solution impossible. The combination of these two factors explains Louis' restless continuation of his acquisitory policy, which was neither unreasonable nor irresponsible. No patriotic French king could rest happy with a frontier still open to Habsburg invasions.

Secondly, while there is much sense in these arguments, one does not have to be an anti-French Protestant propagandist to argue that Louis' methods unnecessarily exacerbated the situation. Dragon's teeth were sown in the 1680s. Indeed, Pomponne, Louis' ex-foreign minister, made precisely this criticism: 'It is true enough that the reunions were based upon the treaty of Munster, but the way in which they were carried out was not always defensible'. Or take the French army's ravaging of the Spanish Low Countries in 1684. Here are Louvois' instructions to his man on the spot:

1 The king having been informed that the Spaniards put to the torch two barns full of fodder and grain situated at the extremities of the villages of Avenelle and Sepmenier, in the administrative district of Avesnes, His Majesty commanded me to inform you that he wishes
5 you to burn twenty villages as close as possible to Charleroi, and that you distribute handbills saying that it is in retaliation for the burning of these two barns; the king's will is that Gauchelys, Guernets, and Fleuru be among their number, and that you take the necessary steps in carrying this out so that not a single house in
10 these twenty villages remains standing; that in the future at the first notification you receive of a similar thing, you will act in like manner without awaiting further orders from His Majesty; that the above should be carried out by a large detachment, which His Majesty wishes you to command yourself, and which is substantial
15 enough so that there need be no fear of the joining of the garrisons of Namur and Charleroi.

The date on which these instructions were issued was 18 February 1684; so innocent and helpless people were to be made homeless in winter.

Even the more harmless manifestations of French imperialism caused resentment. The monument in the Place des Victoires which commemorated the peace of Nymegen offended both friend and foe. So did the Paris city gates which were transformed into triumphal arches in the Roman style; their bas-reliefs depicted Louis in the guise of the god Hercules, conquering his enemies. Charles XII of Sweden despised Louis for allowing statues of himself to be displayed. An English diplomat criticised 'this Great Comet which is risen of late, the French King, who expects not only to be gazed at but adored by the whole world'. Nor did everybody enthuse over the widespread Gallomania. A contemporary German wrote disapprovingly: 'Today everything has to be French - language, clothes, food, music, illnesses. The majority of the German courts live in the French style, and whoever wants to make a career there must know French and above all have been to Paris'.

To sum up, France's position when the truce of Ratisbon was signed was immensely strong. The combination of natural resources, luck and skill had paid dividends. However, it cannot be said that Louis XIV and his people had handled success with the restraint and sensitivity which ideally they should have displayed. The cynicism of the reunions, the king's exploitation of the emperor's involvement against the Turks, the devastations wrought by the French army built up widespread resentment. The King of France and his great country might be admired, but the French were also distrusted and feared. Perhaps a fair comparison might be with the domination of the western world by America after the Second World War: the same cultural aggression, the same arrogance, the same stampede by everyone else to copy American models. No American leader quite filled the role of Louis XIV; perhaps J.F.Kennedy might have done, given time. Like the Americans the French were soon to experience their Vietnam.

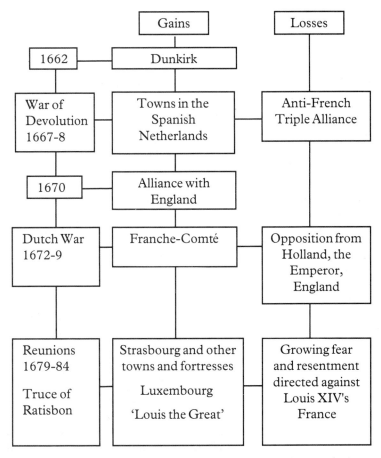

Summary: Louis XIV and Foreign Affairs, 1661-84

CHAPTER 7

Louis XIV and Foreign Affairs - The Later Years, 1684 - 1715

1 The Origins of the Nine Years War

The last quarter century of Louis XIV's reign was to be dominated by war. France was to be involved in conflict with a wide-ranging European alliance determined to cancel all the previous achievements of Louis' foreign policy. There were to be no more easy victories for the Sun King's military machine; indeed, France would soon be fighting for her life. The domestic reforms of Colbert, the administrative advances of Louvois, and the cultural marvels of the reign were all put at risk by these wars. Hundreds of thousands died in battle and millions starved - both in France and throughout Europe.

What caused this cataclysmic tragedy? Was it the inevitable result of the Sun King's megalomania as his critics have maintained? Was it a case of the powers of Europe saying 'enough is enough' and combining at last against the French bully? Or, as Louis' defenders have argued, was France the victim of envy and resentment? Was it that Louis' enemies could not see that his 'robust foreign policy' (Bluche) was defensive and not offensive, designed to make war less likely?

First the outbreak of the costly, inconclusive war which lasted from 1688 to 1697 must be explained. This used to be known as the War of the League of Augsburg, but historians now call it the Nine Years War.

Louis XIV did not want this war, but he brought it upon himself by his paranoia over national security. Certainly during the late 1680s Louis became more apprehensive. He was increasingly aware that the balance of power was tilting against France. This was partly because the emperor was mastering his problems in eastern Europe - gradually recovering control over Hungary, and in August 1687 winning the great battle of Mohacs against the Turks. Soon his battle-hardened troops would be redeployed in western Europe. 'The Germans must from now on be considered our real enemies', Louvois grimly remarked to Vauban who increasingly concentrated his defensive skills on France's eastern frontier. Louvois was proved right when in July 1686 the Emperor and several German princes combined with Sweden and Spain to form the League of Augsburg in order to counter French aggression.

Meanwhile, France was hard hit by a trade recession and disastrous harvests. Colbert's conscientious successor, Le Peletier, demanded cuts in government expenditure. Louis therefore could afford less than 50 million livres a year on the army and fortifications during the period 1685-7, as against 70 million between 1680 and 1684. Furthermore, the troops' health and discipline were undermined by Louvois' policy of employing them on constructing palaces and diverting rivers for fountains. New ships could not be afforded for the navy. France was losing the technological war as well. Huguenot exiles had betrayed the secret of the bomb-ketch to the English and Dutch, while there was neither time nor money to equip the French army with the improved flintlock musket and the socket-bayonet.

It is against this background of anxiety and pessimism that Louis' actions must be evaluated. Two particular concerns were Philippsburg and Cologne. Philippsburg was in imperial hands and menaced lower Alsace, especially Strasburg which was Louis' most treasured acquisition. All Vauban's preparations were at risk until Philippsburg was French. The Archbishopric of Cologne was equally crucial. It was a Catholic outpost in Protestant territory. It was geographically and strategically vital, for example, providing Louis XIV with access to Holland in 1672. Since Mazarin's time the Archbishop of Cologne had been a French stooge, and the present incumbent, Maximilian-Henry of Wittelsbach, was wholly reliable, being kept in line by his pro-French assistant William-Egon von Furstenberg. But Maximilian-Henry was elderly and could not be expected to live for very much longer.

Unfortunately for France, Louis XIV compounded his problems by adding a religious dimension. First, in October 1685 he revoked the Edict of Nantes, cancelling the toleration which French Protestants had enjoyed since 1598. Protestant writers have exaggerated the results of this measure (see page 65), but it was certainly a gift to anti-French propagandists in Germany, Holland and Britain. It also caused the emigration of tens of thousands of Protestant soldiers and sailors who joined France's enemies. Secondly, Louis involved himself in a long, damaging quarrel with the papacy. This quarrel descended to new depths in November 1687 when, on Louis' orders, the French ambassador refused to co-operate with the Vatican's campaign to root out criminals exploiting diplomatic immunity. Pope Innocent XI retaliated by publicly excommunicating the French ambassador and preparing for Louis' own excommunication. Louis counter-attacked with propaganda, alleging that the Pope's anti-French prejudices amounted to madness. In addition, as he was too ready to do, the Eldest Son of the Church resorted to violence against the Holy Father. Louis sent a thrill of horror through Catholic Europe by seizing the papal state of Avignon in southern France.

The full folly of Louis XIV's conflict with Rome became apparent on 3 June 1688 when Maximilian-Henry, the Archbishop of Cologne, inconveniently died. For not only had the new archbishop's appointment to be confirmed by the Pope, but also in the event of a disputed election the Pope had the final say. Louis' candidate was the French pensioner, von Furstenberg. Equally inevitably the imperialists put up a candidate - the 17-year-old Joseph-Clement of Bavaria, the Elector's brother. In the event, the cathedral chapter voted inconclusively and the case therefore went to Rome.

It must be re-emphasised that from Louis XIV's point of view this was no storm in an ecclesiastical teacup. French security hung on the Cologne election. Louis therefore applied himself to winning over the papacy. His normal reaction would have been to bribe the Pope. But, alas, Innocent XI was notoriously incorruptible. Louis therefore tried to appease Innocent. He sent a trusted negotiator, the marquis de Chamlay, to offer concessions and to explain why the Pope should support the French candidate. He was to point out to the Pope that the imperial candidate was only 17, while on the other hand Furstenberg was an experienced and suitably qualified churchman. In addition Chamlay was to convey the following message from his master:

1 Any refusal by His Holiness to grant the necessary bulls would only serve to set off a war in the Empire which it would be hard to end, and which would cause Christendom to lose all those advantages which have been secured only because I have not wished to profit
5 from favourable circumstances to press the claims of my Crown against neighbouring states ... while the Emperor's forces were occupied in Hungary.

We shall never know how effective this not particularly subtle approach would have been, for the Pope flatly refused to see Chamlay. Louis therefore prepared to use force. A French cardinal was instructed to read to the Pope a manifesto announcing the imminent arrival of a French army in Italy which would punish the Pope for his unreasonable attitude; the Pope was entirely to blame for any bloodshed which resulted. Innocent XI listened carefully to the manifesto and two days later, on 18 September 1688, conferred the Archbishopric of Cologne on the youthful Joseph-Clement.

Louis had by now made up his mind that force was the only answer to his various problems. The Italian invasion was in fact postponed in favour of military action on France's eastern frontiers where the most acute danger was perceived to be. Louis published another self-justifying manifesto, this time addressed to the Emperor. The Most Christian King was about to take up arms reluctantly, with intentions that were entirely defensive; all he wanted was that the truce of Ratisbon should be made permanent. He regretted having to appeal to arms while the Emperor was still fighting the Turks. If however war resulted, it was all the fault of France's enemies, notably the Pope, the Emperor and the German princes. Louis gave his enemies until January 1689 to agree to meaningful negotiations.

There is no need to question Louis' sincerity in claiming that his intentions were defensive, that he wished to negotiate, that he would be happy with his enemies' confirmation of the Ratisbon settlement. But he blundered by issuing threats which were decreasingly effective. And he now spoilt his case by resorting to force before the ultimatum which he had given his enemies had run out. Undoubtedly this new initiative was intended to be another limited operation, designed to make a major war less likely, not more likely. But Louis XIV provoked the war he was trying to avoid.

At first everything went well for the French. In late September 1688 they laid siege to Philippsburg which was taken on 29 October. This was a spectacular achievement. Furthermore, there was a succession of French victories in the Palatinate. Although Cologne itself could not be taken, several important places, such as Mannheim, Heidelberg and, further south, the Archbishopric of Trier, were occupied. France's eastern frontier was now more secure than it had ever been.

However, these undoubted successes were overshadowed by William of Orange's amazing campaign in England. French intelligence was aware that this expedition was a possibility. Throughout the summer of 1688 William had shrewdly deployed his army at Nymegen to keep the French guessing, for he was well placed either to interfere with French plans on the Rhine or equally to move against Louis' ally the King of England. When Louis finally committed himself by attacking Philippsburg, there was relief in the Dutch camp. On 8 October William persuaded the States-General to support his invasion of England. On 11 November he set sail. By the end of the year he had landed, neutralised the English armed forces, run his father-in-law out of the country and arranged for himself and his wife to be crowned as joint monarchs of England. The balance of power was transformed.

Louis XIV has been criticised for allowing William's invasion and the resulting 'Glorious Revolution' to happen. Certainly with hindsight it is clear that Louis should have maintained his threat against the United Provinces in order to deter an invasion of England, for Louis' ally James II proved to be incapable of looking after himself. Indeed, if Louis had been really clever, should he not have invaded Holland in the autumn of 1688 rather than in the spring of 1672?

But Louis XIV does not deserve this criticism. His decision to mount a German offensive and leave William of Orange to his own devices was realistic. No-one could have predicted the events which now unfolded in England, for all the odds were against William succeeding. To have evaded the English navy, to have shepherded his cumbersome armada through the November storms (what a time of year to choose!), to have landed on an enemy-occupied coastline (the most difficult military operation from Caesar to Montgomery) - all this defied prediction. Similarly, when James II crowned a dazzling display of ineptitude by running away, obligingly leaving the kingdom to the usurper, Louis was understandably astonished as well as dismayed. He had had every right to doubt whether William, normally extremely cautious, would invade at all, whether he would safely arrive, whether he would succeed in achieving a satisfactory settlement with James II (for he could hardly offer violence to his wife's father) or with the xenophobic English.

Where Louis XIV definitely did blunder was to magnify his problems in a manner which had become only too typical. In order to straighten his defensive frontier Louis accepted Louvois' advice not only to pull out of the Palatinate but also to devastate it. Between December 1688 and May 1689 this unfortunate part of Germany, including Worms, Speyer and Heidelberg was razed to the ground. The effect of this rational but ruthless policy was disastrous so far as German public opinion was concerned. War is always an ugly business, but this perpetration of deliberate atrocities was perceived to be above conventional wartime frightfulness. Bluche points out that other military commanders, such as Charles XII of Sweden and Marlborough, also resorted to similar tactics. But contemporaries believed that Louis started it.

Nevertheless, when the origins of the Nine Years War are considered, Louis must be acquitted of the charge of deliberately provoking it. He was neither a warmonger nor a megalomaniac. He did not aim at world monarchy or even at the domination of Europe. Still less did he want the long and expensive war which materialised. His thinking was genuinely defensive, his objectives reasonable and in France's true interests. The real charge against the Sun King is that he was inept. For during these years Louis never grasped the impact of his actions on others. He failed to see how patently dishonest the justifications for the reunions were. He could not appreciate how hollow his self-congratulation must appear to be for exercising restraint while the Emperor was locked in his life-and-death struggle with the Turks. The devastation of the Palatinate had consequences that he never realised. likewise his attempts to bully the Pope. Louis was too ready to resort to force and to grab yet more territory; these were the short-cuts which would always solve his problems. When Bluche argues that 'unlike William of Orange, Louis did not have the plunderer's instinct', contemporaries would have replied, 'You could have fooled us'.

2 The Nine Years War, 1688-97

The Nine Years War was a dreadful war - an inconclusive slogging match which brought widespread death and destruction. A hideous stalemate prevailed over the blood-soaked battlefields of Flanders. And while opportunities for decisive action existed at sea, neither high command had the vision to seize them. However, a decision of sorts was certainly achieved in the British Isles. William of Orange, now William III, successfully fought off challenges to his precarious throne. Rebellions mounted by Jacobites (supporters of the exiled James II) were snuffed out in Scotland, while an Irish challenge, led by James in person and supported by Louis XIV, was also a failure.

Louis' treatment of James II shows him at his best and at his worst. No-one could have been kinder than Louis to the fallen monarch. Out of compassion for a man down on his luck and out of solidarity for a fellow king, Louis presented James with the palace of Saint-Germain and the cash to run it. 'Here is your home', said Louis to James. 'When I come here, you will be my host just as I shall be yours when you come to Versailles'. On the other hand, Louis showed defective judgement by supporting James's attempts to recover his throne. The French courtiers 'read' James II: 'when you speak to him, you realise why he is here'. Louis XIV on the other hand clearly regarded James II as a good bet; and like a hooked gambler, he squandered money, men and time on a lost cause. Louis listened far too much to James and his fellow exiles who lost touch with England but continued to believe that a Jacobite restoration was round the next corner.

In 1689-90 Louis XIV invested money, men and ships, which could well have been committed elsewhere, in the Irish campaign. Although the French navy gave a creditable account of itself in the battles of Bantry Bay and Beachy Head, James II proved to be an inept leader, the Catholic Irish fought inconsistently and William III won the crucial battle of the Boyne (10 July 1690). 'The Irish ran away!' shouted James II as he galloped into Dublin. 'But Your Majesty has run even faster', retorted one of the court ladies. At great risk the French navy brought James and his followers back to Saint-Germain.

Meanwhile, France was faced with a formidable continental coalition, the First Grand Alliance. The Dutch declared war in November 1688. Within six months they had been joined by the Empire, Brandenburg, Spain, England and Bavaria. Savoy became a member of the coalition in June 1690. Mathematically France was outnumbered: 220,000 fighting men against 150,000. However, France possessed the advantage of a unified command, whereas the coalition of her enemies was handicapped by mutual distrust, confusion and conflicting aims. Louis XIV brought Luxembourg out of disgrace and he proved to be the best general on either side. In addition, his army was efficiently administered by Louvois and his navy by Seignelay. By contrast the lynchpin of the coalition was William of Orange. 'Brave, brave, by heaven he deserves a crown!' exclaimed his Englishmen when William led them into battle. But he was an unimaginative and unlucky strategist, plagued by inadequate subordinates and poorly trained troops; he must be one of the most frequently defeated generals in history.

Louis XIV's soldiers fought reasonably successful campaigns in Italy and Spain. But in Flanders, the most important theatre, dreary stalemate prevailed. There was 'much marching and counter-marching', as the cliché goes, while the rival high-commands besieged each-others' fortresses. The French armies under Louis' personal direction captured Namur in 1692, but due to the incompetence of the French commander Villeroy, William III recaptured it three years later - perhaps his greatest military achievement. Luxembourg defeated William III at Steenkirk and Neerwinden which gave Louis XIV 'enormous satisfaction'; but they were not decisive victories.

The most dramatic events took place at sea. Until May 1692 the French fleet commanded by Tourville dominated the Channel. But a land-based committee of 'experts' including James II implied that Tourville was a coward and morally blackmailed him into accepting battle off Cape La Hague with a superior English fleet. The French were outclassed. James II, forgetting which side he was now supposed to support, could not resist applauding the expertise of the English fleet which in happier days he had himself commanded. When the defeated admiral reported to Versailles, the courtiers expected him to be castigated. But Louis XIV was not a mean employer:

> I am happy with your conduct and with all the navy; we have been defeated, but you have earned glory, both for yourself and for the nation. It has cost us some ships, but this will be put right during the coming year, and assuredly we will defeat the enemy.

And so it proved. After receiving a marshal's baton, Tourville won the battle of Lagos in 1693 as a result of which 75 Dutch ships were destroyed or captured. In the following year the ex-pirate Jean Bart drove off a stronger Dutch escorting force and captured a convoy of 30 grain ships - the first of two French naval victories at the Texel. A medal commemorating the victory claimed: 'France supplied with wheat by the king, after the defeat of a Dutch squadron'. These were great days for the French navy; at the end of the war it boasted 137 ships of the line. During the course of the war the French claimed to have captured or destroyed over 5,000 English and Dutch merchantships.

But in truth France lacked wheat. The winters of 1693 and 1694 had been severe. The peasants were ruined by taxation. Louis was at his wit's end as to how to finance further campaigns. In 1696 he split his enemies by making peace with Savoy; Casale and Pinerolo were surrendered and the king's grandson, the duc de Burgundy, married a Savoyard princess. This diplomatic coup shook the Coalition, whose members were almost as exhausted as France. A peace conference opened at Ryswick in May 1697 and terms were agreed in September.

By the Treaty of Ryswick Louis XIV retained French Hainault, but surrendered his other gains in Flanders acquired since 1678. Similarly he gave up Luxembourg and Philippsburg, although he was allowed to keep Lower Alsace including Strasbourg. He returned Lorraine to its duke and Avignon to the Pope. He had to admit his failure to control Cologne. In other words, with the exception of Strasbourg, France lost all Louis' acquisitions achieved since the peace of Nymegen as a result of the reunions and his other offensives. France also returned Barcelona to Spain and her Canadian conquests to England. Louis had the mortification of having to recognise William of Orange as 'His Majesty William III, King of Great Britain'.

Bluche praises Louis XIV for his moderation and readiness to make peace. He quotes Louis' satisfaction at the conclusion of the treaty:

1 Strasbourg, one of the principal ramparts of the empire and of heresy, united forever with the Church and with my crown; the Rhine established as the barrier between France and Germany; and, most important to me, the practice of the true religion
5 authorised by a solemn engagement entered into by sovereigns of different religions, these are the gains of the recent treaty.

It was indeed the case that German princes were prepared to grant Catholicism the toleration which Louis denied Protestantism. However, Bluche seems to have accepted French propaganda at face value. The truth was that France was too exhausted to continue the war. Furthermore, all eyes were on Madrid where Carlos II was at last really dying; Louis wanted his decks cleared for action.

As for France's enemies, they emerged from the Nine Years War with other gains which were less tangible than those recorded at Ryswick but which were just as important. It was immensely significant that French arrogance and aggression had at last been checked. Of even greater importance, the alliance had functioned unevenly but surprisingly effectively. If necessary it could be reactivated. Above all, William III had acted as midwife to the birth of a great power. Britain was no longer an off-shore island which the continental powers could patronise or ignore. Her armed forces had played a major role in a European war. Although he was no military genius himself, William had discovered and promoted Marlborough - who was a genius. This was especially perceptive of the king as he neither liked nor trusted Marlborough. William had 'blooded' the English army, improving its equipment and supporting arms such as artillery and medical services. It would indeed be a formidable opponent if another round had to be fought. Lastly the foundation of the Bank of England and the establishment of the national debt in 1694 had enabled the government to borrow at low-interest rates. Now, in contrast to France, major wars could be funded without resource to high-interest borrowing and the large-scale sale of office. Furthermore, by investing in the Bank of England the English were committed to the anti-Jacobite cause; where their treasure was, there were their hearts also.

Louis XIV had convinced a wide spectrum of European opinion that it was necessary to resist France. This is the explanation of both the formation and the durability of the First Grand Alliance which had now fought France to a standstill and extracted the Treaty of Ryswick. English gentry and Dutch merchants followed William of Orange in his anti-French crusade not out of love for him but because they felt that it was in their interests to do so. And the same situation prevailed in Germany. Nothing was more significant than Colbert de Croissy's failure to revive a French party of German princes between 1689 and 1693. Over six million livres were spent in this sensible attempt to split France's enemies. But, like the English and the Dutch, the Germans now feared the King of France. Protestants were alienated by the persecution of the Huguenots, Catholics by Louis' quarrel with Rome. All Germans recalled the reunions and the devastation of the Palatinate. It was against this background that Louis XIV addressed himself to the Spanish succession.

3 From Ryswick to the Hague, 1697-1702

For five years after the signing of the peace of Ryswick the Spanish succession dominated Europe. Carlos the Sufferer's existence of living death, which had defied medical science for so long (see page 95), was coming to a close. The unfortunate man was now suffering from dropsy. However, he was once more to prove his ability to surprise his contemporaries. In a will made shortly before he died on All Saints' Day 1700 Carlos II handed over to Louis XIV everything that ambitious monarch had angled for over the previous half century.

Controversy has raged ever since about whether Louis XIV reacted by scoring a decisive and dramatic own goal. For Louis now took steps which outraged his old enemies, the powers of the Grand Alliance. Another long and disastrous war followed, culminating in the division of the Spanish empire. However, some historians have argued that this war was unavoidable and that Louis' admittedly clumsy and insensitive measures actually made little difference. To understand these issues, it is essential to grasp the sequence of events between the Peace of Ryswick and the outbreak of the War of the Spanish Succession. There is a summary in an appendix at the end of this section.

Until Carlos II died, Louis XIV acted with great discretion. This was partly because France was too exhausted for an aggressive or risky policy to make sense. Furthermore, Louis was influenced by the shrewd and cautious Colbert de Torcy, who was secretary of state for foreign affairs from 1698 to 1715. Torcy, yet another member of the Colbert dynasty, was in addition Pomponne's son-in-law, so diplomacy was certainly part of his background. As Louis aged, Torcy took on more and more of the day-to-day administration of France's foreign policy, not only forging the king's signature but also his handwriting. Nevertheless, Louis never relaxed his grip on major decisions.

There is no need to question the sincerity of Louis' wish to avoid further conflict, or for that matter William III's. The problem was quite clearly that Carlos II would shortly die, leaving no heir; nor were there any other legitimate members of the Spanish royal family who could succeed. Two European royal families claimed the Spanish throne - the Austrian Habsburgs and the French Bourbons. Although Spain was no longer the international force that she had once been, the extent and the wealth of her empire was vast: Spain, the Indies, much of Italy and the Spanish Low Countries. If either dynasty acquired the whole of the Spanish empire, the European balance of power would be overturned. Both William and Louis appreciated this and therefore tried to arrange a partition which would preserve the peace of Europe.

The first partition treaty of October 1698 was admirably realistic. The Emperor Leopold's grandson, Joseph Ferdinand of Bavaria, was to receive the lion's share - Spain, the Indies, the Low Countries and Sardinia; the Archduke Charles, Leopold's second son, was to receive Milan; and the Dauphin was to inherit other Italian territories, which Louis would certainly attempt to use as bargaining counters in order to improve the *pré carré*. The great attraction of this solution was that Joseph Ferdinand's father was a Wittelsbach, and therefore neither France nor the Empire would be strengthened. Unfortunately a few months later Joseph Ferdinand died of smallpox.

So Louis and William had to begin again, but now against a more difficult background. Leopold had signed the peace of Karlowitz (26 January 1699) which finally freed him from the Turkish menace and enabled him to concentrate on western Europe. He had strongly disapproved of any plans to split the Spanish empire. So had Carlos II - and indeed it might have been wiser to have involved the Habsburg courts rather more in the discussions. Nevertheless, undaunted, Torcy and pensionary Heinsius on behalf of Louis XIV and William III got to work again and hammered out the second partition treaty. The Archduke Charles was to receive Spain, the Indies and the Low Countries; the Dauphin's share was to be all the Italian lands with the exception of Milan which was to go to the Duke of Lorraine who would hand his duchy over to France. When the details of the treaty were divulged to the Emperor and to Carlos II, both firmly refused to accept it. This unsatisfactory situation prompted the King of Spain to make a will.

When Carlos II died, the contents of his will hit Europe like a bombshell. He left his whole empire to Philip, duc d'Anjou, Louis XIV's grandson, with the stipulation that the thrones of France and Spain were never to be united. If Philip refused this glittering inheritance, it was to go to the Archduke Charles. There is absolutely no reason to doubt Louis XIV's astonishment, for Carlos II had always loathed the Sun King. Indeed, the French ambassador once reported that Carlos's hatred of France amounted to insanity. His court was equally paranoid in its hatred of everything French. Louis XIV's niece, Marie Louise, Carlos II's first wife, had been given a terrible time. Letters were forged to prove that she was having an affair with a guardsman, her parrots were strangled because they spoke French, and she herself was eventually poisoned. Probably Carlos left everything to Philip of Anjou for one reason only; he presumably reckoned that France could most effectively defend the Spanish empire. 'I had always thought that Spain was on our side; I never expected them to call in the French', was an understandable Dutch comment.

All eyes were now on Versailles to see what the French reaction would be. For a week Louis XIV carefully weighed the alternatives. Torcy argued against accepting the will on the grounds that the king would be accused by the maritime powers of breaking his word and that a European war would result. The Dauphin, Pontchartrain (the chancellor) and Madame de Maintenon - in whose rooms the discussions took place - disagreed. They argued that there was no point in handing the Spanish empire over to the Habsburgs; that if the French decided to accept a war would not necessarily result; and that there would be the considerable financial advantages to be gained from 'inundating Latin America with Breton cloth and ebony [slaves from French west Africa]'.

In the end Louis summoned the Spanish ambassador and invited him to greet the duc d'Anjou as his king. 'The Pyrenees are no more!' exclaimed the Spaniard. Flinging open the doors, Louis presented his grandson to the courtiers with the words, 'Gentlemen, here is the King of Spain'. The die was cast - or so it might appear.

But this is where the sequence of events is crucial, for there is the possibility that if Louis had played his cards with restraint, war might have been avoided. It is a fact that both England and Holland promptly recognised Philip V. It is a fact that public opinion in Holland and England dreaded a renewal of war: 'the people here remain as stupid as ever', William reported from London in disgust. Perhaps if Louis had appreciated the importance of public opinion in London and the Hague, perhaps if he had understood William's and Leopold's personalities, he might have avoided the mistakes which he now made. But Louis never visited London and never met his fellow monarchs. Whatever the explanation the Sun King now committed three unnecessary blunders. First, on his instructions, the *parlement* of Paris recorded that Philip V had by no means renounced his claim to the French throne. Louis' motive was probably to keep his brother's family away from the succession, rather than to create the possibility of a new superpower; but Europe shuddered. Next, on behalf of his grandson, Louis expelled the Dutch troops from their barrier fortresses in the Spanish Netherlands; the Dutch were horrified. Lastly James II was dying. Louis, influenced by Madame de Maintenon and reflecting that only God can set aside the rules of hereditary succession, cheered his old client's deathbed by recognising his son as James III. It is hard to think of a surer way of provoking English hostility.

How damaging were these provocative measures? Louis' defenders have pointed out that the Grand Alliance of the Hague, the coalition which was to bring France to her knees, was formed *before* Louis recognised James III, and that therefore Louis' gesture in James III's favour did not cause the war. This is true. But it is uncertain whether the

Grand Alliance would necessarily have gone to war. William might well have been in favour of such action but as King of England he was no longer a free agent. For he had been obliged to sign the Act of Settlement which drastically curtailed the monarch's freedom of manoeuvre. During the meetings at the Hague when the Grand Alliance was formed, William had to refer questions about England's military commitment back to London. English public opinion therefore was crucial.

Furthermore, there is another consideration. Diplomats at the Hague were appalled by William III's appearance. When the anaemic Dutchman arrived leaning on the arm of the youthful-looking Duke of Marlborough observers could hardly believe that the two men were the same age. A few weeks later William was dead. While Louis could not predict this, William's poor health was reported at Versailles. Why provoke the alliance of France's enemies when its mainspring was about to fail? Treated with circumspection this alliance bereft of its leader might well disintegrate. But it was not to be. Insensitivity reaped its reward. On 15 May 1702 the Grand Alliance declared war on France.

How culpable was Louis XIV? One can certainly exaggerate the case against him. No doubt sheer greed played its part in prompting the powers who formed the Grand Alliance to dispute the Spanish succession, a factor which would have operated in any case. But it is impossible to maintain that Louis' conduct of foreign policy since the publication of Carlos II's will showed great intelligence.

Events 1697-1702

October	1697	The Peace of Ryswick.
October	1698	First partition treaty between France, England, and Holland.
February	1699	Death of the electoral prince of Bavaria.
March	1700	Second partition treaty.
November	1700	Death of Charles II. Louis XIV accepted the will.
February	1701	*Parlement* asserted Philip's rights to the French throne. French occupation of the barrier fortresses.
June	1701	Act of Settlement curtailed William's freedom of action.
September	1701	The Grand Alliance of the Hague signed. Death of James II. Louis recognised James III.
8 May	1702	Death of William III.
15 May	1702	The Empire, England, Holland declared war on France.

4 The War of the Spanish Succession, 1702-13

Another decade of war and suffering was now to be inflicted on Europe. It was soon to be clear that generals had rediscovered the art of winning battles. Yet not even the genius of Marlborough could make it a wholly decisive war. In the end yet more futility resulted. Certainly not much was decided in the first two years of the war, for the sides were too well matched. While the French navy had declined, the army was in good shape. It was equipped with the socket-bayonet and the flintlock musket, and Louis had raised more regiments. At the height of the war the French army numbered 400,000 men - an astonishing feat of organisation. The allies could raise 250,000 and were better co-ordinated than in the previous war thanks to the diplomatic skill of Marlborough. The advantages of French unified command were balanced by the success of the allies in isolating France. After Savoy and Portugal went over to the allies in 1703, Louis and his grandson had only the Elector of Bavaria as an ally.

Indecisive campaigns in Italy, the Low Countries and Bavaria highlighted the conflict on both sides between caution and enterprise. Villars had successfully defended Bavaria by defeating the imperialists at Friedlingen and Hoechstadt, but he was unable to conceal his contempt for the Elector of Bavaria's timidity and had to be recalled. Marlborough manoeuvred skilfully in the bishopric of Cologne but was driven to distraction by the Dutch who refused permission for their troops to leave their own backyard.

Only by bold initiatives could the war be won; this was Marlborough's conviction. If the Dutch would not agree to the invasion of France, then they would have to digest an even bolder strategy. Marlborough devised a plan to kidnap the Anglo-Dutch army and lead it to the other side of Europe; there he would combine with the imperialists to win that decisive victory which had so far eluded both sides. The plan worked. Marlborough led his forces down the Scheldt and then to the bewilderment of the Dutch headed for south Germany where he met Eugène. Together they could face the equally numerous host of the French and Bavarians. The armies met near the hamlet of Blenheim on the banks of the Danube (13 August 1704).

Blenheim was a turning-point in military and political history. Marlborough appreciated that the deployment of the Franco-Bavarian army was unsound while his battle plan was a classic exercise in forcing the enemy to lose his balance while retaining one's own. Eugène played a crucial role in pinning down the Bavarians on the opposing left wing. Marlborough himself launched the British infantry in a ferocious attack on the French right, based on the village of Blenheim. Tallard now made the mistake of committing his reserve to the defence of Blenheim - exactly as Marlborough had hoped. Meanwhile Marlborough had nibbled away at the centre, capturing the bridges over the stream.

Through this weakened centre he now launched the cavalry which swept the opposition aside and wheeled left, entrapping the French right. Twelve thousand Frenchmen surrendered, including Tallard who was to be imprisoned in Nottingham. There he endeared himself to the local gentry by introducing them to celery.

Blenheim was simply not believed at Versailles until the truth was confirmed. Certainly, the Sun King's armies had been checked before. But the idea of a French army being thrashed and its commander taken prisoner was difficult to assimilate. No-one dared tell the king and it was left to Madame de Maintenon to break it to him that, in Saint-Simon's words, 'he was no longer invincible'. On the battlefield the victors left a monument with the legend: 'Let Louis XIV acknowledge that no man should be called happy or great before his death'.

As a result of Blenheim Bavaria was overrun and devastated by the allies and the military prestige of France was irreparably damaged. At the same time Gibraltar had been captured by the British and in the next few months the Archduke Charles invaded Catalonia and Valencia. In the winter of 1705-6 Louis XIV put out peace-feelers - Spain for the archduke, Lorraine and part of the Spanish Netherlands for France. The allies agreed with Heinsius that Louis' offer should be rejected.

Indeed, 1706 was to bring the Sun King's fortunes lower still. His armies were defeated - thrice. In May Marlborough won the battle of Ramillies against Villeroy, a courtier whom Louis had promoted because he was so servile; it was said that women found him irresistible, but the enemy were less convinced. As at Blenheim the French army was badly deployed. Marlborough fooled Villeroi into committing his reserves on his left wing, then withdrew troops from that part of the battle (what arrogant versatility!) in order to redeploy them against the French centre and right. A Danish cavalry charge made it a cosmopolitan triumph. '"God seems to have forgotten all I have done for him", was Louis' dumbfounded comment. Flanders and Brabant were lost to France.' A few weeks later Eugène won the battle of Turin and followed it up by throwing the French out of Italy. Meanwhile, Philip V was expelled from Madrid where on 25 June 1706 the archduke was proclaimed Charles III.

As a matter of fact Bourbon fortunes now began to pick up in Spain. The archduke found it impossible to work with his English allies, Louis sent capable administrators and generals to help his grandson and the Spanish, as ever a proud race, reflected that their king had made a will in favour of Philip V. Furthermore, the archduke was assisted by heretics, who made no attempt to conceal their contempt for the Catholic faith. Horror stories reached Versailles about the enormities of the blasphemous English; a shocked Louis XIV recounted these to the Spanish ambassador who rubbed his hands and exclaimed, 'excellent, excellent - the more the better'.

But the nadir was yet to be reached in the north. The king interfered by appointing both the duc de Burgundy and the duc de Vendôme to command the French army. Burgundy was inexperienced, but was the king's grandson; Vendôme was a professional who did not take kindly to amateur interference. The king could not make up his mind who was in charge, so the result was chaos. Marlborough exploited the situation at Oudenaarde (11 July 1708). Unlike Blenheim and Ramillies which had been set-piece battles, this was an improvised, running fight. Marlborough did not give the French the chance to sort themselves out but attacked at once; the duc de Burgundy compounded French chaos by ordering a retreat towards Ghent, thus turning a shambles into a catastrophe. The fall of Lille and the invasion of France followed.

Louis XIV and his people now suffered further torment: the winter of 1708-9. Partridges froze in the fields, the wine froze at Versailles, in Paris 24,000 people perished from cold. Alternating thaws and further severe frosts destroyed the crops. Famine stared France in the face; crowds of beggars threatened public order. Louis commented: 'It is very easy to govern a kingdom from an office with a decree: but when one has to defy half of Europe after the loss of five great battles and the atrocious winter of 1709, it is not so simple'.

Against this background of defeat and disaster France's return to the negotiating table was logical. Indeed, Louis was now absolutely frantic for war to end. He went to unprecedented lengths to satisfy his enemies. Contrary to custom he sent Torcy in person - a royal minister - to negotiate on his behalf. Torcy was instructed to agree to the withdrawal of Philip V from the Spanish throne, the surrender of Strasbourg and territory in Flanders, the recognition of Queen Anne, William III's Protestant successor to the English throne, and the expulsion from France of James III and his followers. Furthermore, despite France's poverty, Torcy was to bribe the Duke of Marlborough:

1 I consent that you should give him a firm assurance that I will pay him two million livres, if through his good offices he can obtain one of the following conditions for me: the cession of Naples and Sicily for the king my grandson, or if the worst comes to the worst, of
5 Naples alone ... I will raise this gratification to three millions if, apart from Naples for my grandson, he can ensure that I retain Dunkirk with its harbour and fortifications. If I should be forced to give way over Dunkirk, I would give him the same sum for obtaining Naples for my grandson and the retention of Strasbourg
10 by me ... Finally you may offer the Duke of Marlborough four millions if he arranges that Naples and Sicily will go to the king my grandson, while I keep Dunkirk with its harbour and fortifications, Strasbourg and Landau.

Given Marlborough's greed, bribery was not such a bad idea. But it did not work. With a mixture of folly and heartlessness, the allies rejected

Louis' offer, insisting that in addition to his other concessions he should agree to assist in expelling his own grandson from Spain. The Dutch were particularly intransigent; perhaps they remembered that Louis had called them 'maggots'.

Louis showed courage in refusing the allies' demands. He also showed flair by addressing his people. The public appeal of 12 June 1709 - even if it was written by Torcy - is to the Sun King's credit:

1 The hope of peace soon is so widespread in my kingdom that I owe it to the fidelity which my people have demonstrated during the course of my reign to inform them of the reasons why they are not yet enjoying the repose which I intended to procure for them. I 5 would have had to accept, in order to achieve this, conditions highly dangerous for the safety of my frontier provinces; but the more I demonstrated a willingness and desire to dissipate the suspicions which my enemies still claimed to have of my powers and intentions, the more they multiplied their demands. I pass over 10 in silence the proposal that I should join my forces with those of the league and force the king, my grandson, to quit his throne ... It is against all humanity they should even conceive of asking me to promise such an alliance with them. Yet even though my affections towards my people are no less great than those I feel for my own 15 children, and even though I share in all the evils which war has inflicted upon such faithful subjects, and though I have demonstrated to the whole of Europe that I want sincerely to give them the contentment of peace, I am certain that they would be opposed to accepting it upon conditions contrary to both the 20 justice and honour of France.

Perhaps inspired by this 'backs to the wall' approach the people of France rallied behind their monarch. Villars proved to be the man of the hour. He provided resolute leadership in the horrible battle of Malplaquet. Technically this was another allied victory as the French army eventually conceded the battlefield to their enemies. But in truth nobody won. At the end of the day 30,000 men from the two sides lay dead or dying. The French had fought with desperate courage and withdrew in good order while the allies were too exhausted by their 'victory' to follow them up. Villars who had fought in the front-lines sustained a shattered knee. In excruciating pain he was carried to Versailles where he received a hero's welcome. The king visited his bedside and the old monarch and his wounded marshal conversed for two hours. Both were sure that the tide had turned.

And so it proved. The winter of 1709-10 was another nightmare for the long-suffering people of France and in 1710 the allies maintained their intransigent attitude towards peace negotiations. However, the fighting in Flanders continued to vindicate the excellence of Vauban's *pré carré;* not even Marlborough could break through. In Spain Philip V's fortunes described an erratic course, but Vendôme eventually achieved the revival of the Bourbon cause. In December 1710 he twice defeated the imperialists. The French navy gave a far better account of itself in the Atlantic than British historians are accustomed to admit, frequently escorting Spanish bullion fleets through the Royal Navy's blockade and capturing a British convoy off Rio de Janeiro.

Finally in July 1712 the resuscitated Villars outmanoeuvred a larger imperial army commanded by Eugène at the battle of Denain. The French achieved tactical surprise as a result of a well-concealed flank-march worthy of Marlborough. Even while the French cavalry were crossing the river behind him, Eugène still failed to realise what was happening and complacently dismissed his staff for lunch. When the assault of Denain began the French carried all before them, capturing eight cannon and all the enemy's flags. This was a crucial success. The Dutch and the imperialists were doing their utmost to spoil the peace negotiations which had opened at Utrecht. The victory of Denain persuaded the Dutch that the days of allied victories were past.

Long before that the luck had begun to turn France's way. First in autumn 1710 the Whig régime in London was replaced by the Tories, committed to ending an unpopular war. Even Marlborough proved to be dispensable. His reputation was shattered by the Tories' leading 'scribbler', Jonathan Swift, and in December 1711 he was sacked. The British foreign secretary meanwhile was in confidential touch with Torcy. Finally in April 1711 the Emperor Joseph I died, leaving his brother the Archduke Charles, to succeed him as the Emperor Charles VI. It made nonsense for Charles's allies to espouse his cause in Spain when success would revive the sixteenth-century Habsburg empire of Charles V which had wrecked the European balance of power.

Peace proved elusive to the last, being delayed by arguments about procedure and precedence, while the Emperor continued to obstruct progress. Nevertheless, on 31 March 1713 treaties were signed between France, Great Britain, Holland, Portugal, Savoy and Brandenburg-Prussia. Charles VI and Philip V continued to oppose any dismemberment of the Spanish empire. Ultimately, however, they too had to submit. Philip V signed a treaty with Britain and Holland on 13 July 1713 and the Emperor signed the treaty of Rastadt with France on 6 March 1714.

5 The Peace Treaties, 1713-14

The issue over which the War of the Spanish Succession had supposedly been fought was decided in favour of the Bourbons: Philip V remained King of Spain. However, he renounced his claim to the French throne so that the threat of a huge Franco-Spanish empire under one ruler was thus expunged. Louis XIV consented to the demolition of the fort at

Dunkirk whence pirates had sallied forth to plague Anglo-Dutch shipping. He recognised the Hanoverians as the rightful successors to the English throne and he again promised to expel the Jacobites. He had to abandon his claims to Luxembourg, Philippsburg, Breisach, Freiburg and Kehl on the eastern frontier and to Menin, Tournai, Furnes and Ypres in the north (see the map on page 107). Namur and Charleroi went to the Elector of Bavaria. Nice was returned to the Duke of Savoy while Lorraine was once again restored to its much-travelled duke. However, Louis retained Lille, Aire and Bethune among his northern conquests and Alsace, including Strasburg, to the east.

The Low Countries which had formerly been Spanish now went to Austria; as did Naples, Sardinia and Milan. Holland retained her barrier fortresses - Furnes, Ypres, Menin, Ghent, Tournai, Mons, Charleroi and Namur. The Scheldt was to remain closed to shipping so that Amsterdam would not be challenged by Antwerp. The Elector of Brandenburg was recognised as King of Prussia and received Spanish Gelderland.

Britain benefited, mostly at the expense of Spain. She gained Gibraltar and Minorca plus the priceless *asiento* - the right to supply the new world colonies with slaves; Britain was to enrich herself throughout the eighteenth century during which approximately three million slaves were to cross the Atlantic in British ships. Britain also received Hudson Bay, Newfoundland, Acadia and St. Kitts from France.

To ask whether the war had been worth it from Louis XIV's point of view might seem the wrong question, since he had been attacked by his enemies and not the other way round; as far as he was concerned it was a defensive war. On the other hand, by his provocative actions after accepting Carlos II's will Louis had to a great extent invited war. If this is admitted, Louis cannot be said to have come out of it well. True, the terms of Utrecht were immeasurably better than the concessions which he offered in 1709 and which the allies in their folly and greed turned down. True, his grandson was still King of Spain, although with a reduced inheritance. However, all France's efforts, sufferings and deprivations had failed to produce viable frontiers. The Dutch got their barrier back again. Louis and his grandson had publicly to accept that the thrones of France and Spain could never be united - even if privately Louis believed that God alone could decide such matters.

What effect did the war have on the European balance of power? In the long run Great Britain gained most. Her vast empire of the eighteenth and nineteenth centuries derived its origins from the wars against Louis XIV and the peace of Utrecht. By contrast, although it was not immediately apparent, Holland was finished as a great power. Paradoxically Spain benefited from shedding many of her overseas commitments; she could now concentrate on reform at home - and she still possessed the riches of the new world. Although Austria gained from the treaties, the rising power was Brandenburg-Prussia.

And what of France? Elsewhere in this book the cost of Louis' wars to the French people is assessed. Suffice it here to quote Voltaire's comment on Louis' 'victories' that 'people died of want to the sound of the *Te Deum*'. However, it should be added that in the context of power politics war, like necessity, is the mother of invention. It is certainly the case that raising, equipping and deploying Louis XIV's armies not only made demands on the French administrative system but extended and developed it. *Le roi bureaucrat* arguably did as much for French military potential as *le roi soleil*. Not that his territorial acquisitions were insignificant. Although the north-eastern frontier was still uneven, France was larger and more compact than in 1661 and had the nucleus of an overseas empire. If Louis' successors wished to play great-power politics, he bequeathed to them vast debts but nevertheless a potentially strong hand.

6 Assessment - Gains and Losses

So ended the Sun King's attempts to put into practice the aims and ideals of his foreign policy. Can we say that he had been successful? Had he served the interests of his people? Had he defended his *gloire* in the widest and best sense? If our verdict is not entirely favourable, how much was Louis to blame? Or was he the victim of circumstances, frustrated by misfortune or the malice of his enemies?

Clearly from Louis' point of view there were creditable achievements. A Bourbon was established on the throne of Spain. The Catholic religion was practised in Strasbourg and tolerated in Protestant Germany. While France had been the sick man of Europe between 1559 and 1661, frequently exploited and invaded, there had been no question of that during Louis' personal rule. Louis had certainly made France more secure by the acquisition of territory and the construction of fortresses. As we have seen, he left a strong hand to his successors.

When we evaluate Louis XIV's foreign policy in detail, the territorial criterion is instructive. How well does Louis XIV's record stand up? Clearly, his achievement was at least respectable. Acquisitions were made which were and still are valuable and important: Franche-Comté, Dunkirk, Alsace (including Strasbourg) and the towns in Flanders - St. Omer, Lille, and Aire. Overseas the foundations of an empire had been laid in America, the West Indies, Africa and the far east.

On the other hand this record could clearly have been better. The list of territories acquired but subsequently relinquished is almost as impressive as Louis XIV's gains. Lorraine was only temporarily abandoned. But what about Charleroi, Menin, Ypres and Tournai? France's northern boundary was still untidy and vulnerable. What about Philippsburg, Breisach, Kehl and Luxembourg? Louis had had these vital strong-points in his grasp and then had been forced to relinquish them. Again, invaluable acquisitions overseas had to be returned to the

British, the Dutch and the Portuguese.

Why did so many gains end up as losses? In the nature of things bargaining occurs at peace conferences and one should not be too hard on Louis for not holding on to all his conquests; indeed, his willingness to compromise was often commendable, as French propaganda was quick to point out. There was, however, a lack of coherence in Louis' approach to his territorial ambitions. Given that the destiny of the Spanish lands on Carlos II's death overshadowed all other European issues, should not France's diplomacy have concentrated on deriving the fullest possible benefit when that happy event occurred? Or if force was to be used, should not the objective have been clearly identified and achieved as quickly and as decisively as possible?. One thinks of Frederick the Great's acquisition of Silesia in 1740; however immoral, the job was done. Should Louis not have overrun the whole of the Spanish Netherlands in 1667 in the same way, thus settling the matter once and for all? He might even have pushed France's eastern and north-eastern frontiers to the Rhine.

Indeed, perhaps the fairest criticism of Louis XIV's conduct of foreign policy is that he was fundamentally second-rate both as a strategist and as a tactician. He certainly does not come across as a far-sighted planner. One's impression is far more of a short-term opportunist, successfully and at times ruthlessly exploiting the weakness of his opponents, or making the most of windfalls offered by fortune or the legal chicanery of his clever advisers. However, his tactical sense was vitiated by a poor grasp of elementary psychology. He consistently failed to anticipate the reactions of his fellow monarchs or of international public opinion. Louis XIV's actions were often a gift to enemy propaganda, so that it was easy to represent him as a would-be world conqueror and to argue that *nec pluribus impar* was quite literally and horrifyingly true.

Louis XIV's tactical insensitivity, especially in the 1680s, provoked the great alliance which first checked and then defeated France. This alliance matched and ultimately surpassed French military and naval resources. The stalemate of the 1690s reflected the fact that the balance of power was shifting to France's disadvantage. In the war of the Spanish succession it became clear that France's enemies had maintained their improvement while France continued to deteriorate. This is the significance of Marlborough's victories which we have therefore described in some detail. Marlborough and Eugene were talented commanders of well-equipped and well-trained troops. The French army at Blenheim, 'which was "commanded" if that is the right word' (Bluche) by Tallard was outclassed. The same happened at Ramillies and Oudenarde. Villeroy was no substitute for Condé, nor could Louis himself direct the war with Louvois' forcefulness and flair. Although France recovered creditably between 1709 and 1713, the cost was horrendous. Furthermore, nothing could conceal the impact of those defeats or the concessions which Louis had to make in 1713.

Louis XIV was not the sole ruler in history to bring disaster on his country through miscalculation. The much-admired Henri IV was only saved by the assassin's knife from international humiliation, while on occasions Richelieu's over-clever diplomacy blew up in his face. One could easily continue the list; Napoleon is perhaps the best example. If Louis has attracted so much blame, it could well be because his personal rule lasted so long; during half a century he was bound to make mistakes, and it was his fate to be still there at the helm when the results of his blunders almost demolished the ship of state.

Revisionist historians do us a valuable service by discouraging hysterical condemnation of Louis XIV, for he surely has suffered from character-assassination. He was certainly not the only warmonger. The Emperor Leopold was at war for 40 out of the 47 years of his reign. Charles XII of Sweden was a warrior to the point of eccentricity, preferring 'to die in battle rather than surrounded by doctors and weeping women'. And William of Orange has more of a case to answer than his admirers admit. There was certainly pressure on self-respecting kings to go to war, and Louis' self-defence is not unreasonable: 'Ambition and glory are always pardonable in a prince'. Furthermore, with all his qualities Louis XIV could not predict the future. It may be apparent to us with the advantage of hindsight that Spain was in decline and that the great days of Dutch imperialism were over. Or again, we tend not to take the Emperor Leopold seriously, though contemporaries credited him with ambition and ability. France's enemies were not paper tigers, who could simply be ignored.

If one were to hazard a judgement, were any of Louis XIV's 'war-crimes' as culpable as his enemies' refusal to make peace in 1709? Bluche and Hatton point out that other contemporary leaders not only went to war but contravened the accepted codes of behaviour. Why should Louis be pilloried for the devastations of Holland and the Palatinate while Marlborough gets away with the rape of Bavaria, to say nothing of war-crimes committed by Charles XII of Sweden and Peter the Great of Russia?

A consensus is emerging among historians that Louis XIV's seemingly offensive foreign policy was in reality a defensively-minded pursuit of France's interests as he saw them. Louis' methods often betrayed a lack of intelligence, sensitivity and moral awareness, while the price which Europe had to pay for his readiness to resort to force and for his miscalculations was high. But the Sun King had his principles, just as he had his achievements.

Making notes on *Louis XIV and Foreign Affairs* (Chapters 6 and 7)

Louis XIV's foreign policy is such a long and complex story that it seemed sensible to break it up into two chapters. Furthermore a good case can be made for regarding the truce of Ratisbon as a watershed, justifying a pause for assessment. However, most exam questions are concerned with Louis' foreign policy as a whole. And clearly the story of France's involvement in European affairs during the personal rule has its own unity. So we shall consider *Louis XIV and Foreign Affairs* in general from the point of view of note taking and essay writing.

To stress the importance of a thorough grasp of the facts when tackling this topic might seem like stating the obvious. Nevertheless, it needs stressing that an incomplete understanding of the overall story will inevitably emerge in your essay writing. Therefore begin by building up a chronological summary of what happened, adding to it as you proceed. Similarly you need to summarise the peace treaties which concluded Louis' various wars. In this context it is essential to be geography-conscious. Refer frequently to the maps on pages 107 and 136.

Examiners sometimes acknowledge the importance of 1684 as a watershed. Therefore summarise the reasons for Louis' success up until that date, and the 'dragon's teeth' which he had sown in the shape of enemies made, public opinion flouted, and provocation given. Again, you might be asked a question about Louis' handling of the Spanish succession between 1697 and 1702. Did Louis throw away the reign's most promising opportunity to achieve his goals without a major war? Be sure to summarise the case for and against Louis' record in this context.

However, the bulk of your note taking should be presentations of the arguments and necessary back-up material on the following topics:
1 Did Louis XIV involve France in too many wars?
2 Was he excessively pre-occupied with his own *gloire?*
3 Did his territorial conquests justify the bloodshed caused by his aggressions?
4 Did Louis XIV display sufficient self-control and realism in his conduct of foreign policy?

Answering essay questions on *Louis XIV and Foreign Affairs*
1 How far did Louis XIV's policies with regard to foreign affairs between 1661 and 1684 create problems which came to the fore between 1684 and 1715?
2 Was Louis XIV's foreign policy betweuen 1661 and 1697 essentially defensive or aggressive?
3 When and why was Louis XIV pre-eminent in Europe? When did this pre-eminence cease?
4 How justifiable is the argument that Louis XIV was responsible for the conflicts in Europe between 1684 and 1713?
5 'Between 1661 and 1684 French foreign policy was conducted with skill and success'. Do you agree?
6 To what extent was Louis XIV's foreign policy actuated by the

pursuit of *la gloire?*

7 'The gains which France made as a result of Louis XIV's wars were negligible'. Discuss.

8 'I have made war too much'. Was Louis XIV fair to himself?

Suppose we briefly consider the last question ('I have made war too much'). This is a fair question, though not as straightforward as it might seem. Avoid at all costs the pitfall of writing narrative; this is what the weak candidate will do - write an account of all Louis' wars leading to a conclusion which will almost certainly begin 'Thus we see that ...'. Barely pass material at best, I am afraid.

So what is the right approach? Perhaps the following suggestions might be helpful. In your introduction you could show that you understand the point of this question. Explain that there is disagreement among historians about whether Louis really was the warmonger of old-fashioned textbooks, revisionists arguing that Louis' wars were justifiable from the point of view of French interests and that some of 'his' wars were imposed on him by his enemies. Avoid giving your own opinion at this stage. In your development section avoid a chronological approach. Instead devote paragraphs to particular propositions which are relevant to the question: for example,'France acquired significant territorial gains which might be thought to justify Louis' wars ...'. There are arguments both for and against Louis' record which you must marshal. Your conclusion could well include the fact that some historians question whether Louis really made the remark in the question. Whether he did or did not, there is certainly a case for the defence. It does not matter how you finally answer the question provided that you do answer it. A carefully-qualified verdict might be the most appropriate.

Source-based questions on *Louis XIV and Foreign Affairs*

1 Louis XIV's Self-Justification

Carefully read Louis XIV's manifesto justifying the War of Devolution (page 99) and his letter to the Pope (page 114). Answer the following questions.

a) Describe the 'tone' of these documents? (3 marks)

b) How far is it possible to believe that Louis XIV really meant what was written in his name in these documents? (6 marks)

c) To what extent do these documents suggest that Louis XIV's aggression was irresponsible and selfish? (5 marks)

d) Who was the intended audience for these documents? (6 marks)

2 The Methods Adopted by Louis XIV to Achieve his Goals

Carefully study Louvois' instructions concerning the devastation of the Low Countries (page 110), Louis XIV's advice to Croissy on how to bribe Marlborough (page 126) and Louis XIV's appeal to the French nation (page 127). Answer the following questions.

a) How far is it possible to explain and excuse the decisions to devastate territory by placing such decisions in context? (5 marks)

b) What light does the attempt to bribe Marlborough and the appeal to the French nation throw on Louis XIV's state of mind towards the end of his reign? (5 marks)

c) Do these three documents suggest that Louis XIV was an opportunist with little consistency of methods or objectives? (5 marks)

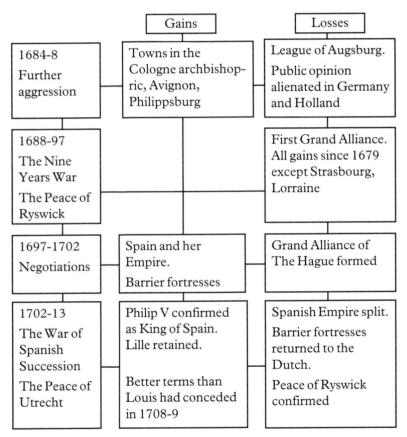

	Gains	Losses
1684-8 Further aggression	Towns in the Cologne archbishop-ric, Avignon, Philippsburg	League of Augsburg. Public opinion alienated in Germany and Holland
1688-97 The Nine Years War The Peace of Ryswick		First Grand Alliance. All gains since 1679 except Strasbourg, Lorraine
1697-1702 Negotiations	Spain and her Empire. Barrier fortresses	Grand Alliance of The Hague formed
1702-13 The War of Spanish Succession The Peace of Utrecht	Philip V confirmed as King of Spain. Lille retained. Better terms than Louis had conceded in 1708-9	Spanish Empire split. Barrier fortresses returned to the Dutch. Peace of Ryswick confirmed

Summary: Louis XIV and Foreign Affairs, 1684 - 1715

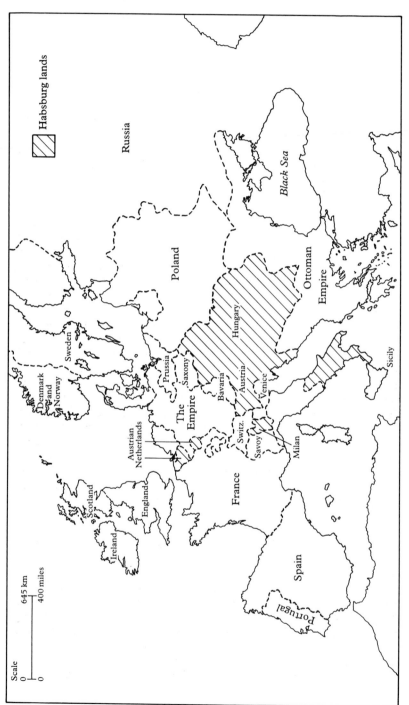

Europe in 1715

CHAPTER 8

Conclusion

1 The End of the Reign

Some biographers of Louis XIV have suggested that his last months were serene and happy. Had not the wars been concluded satisfactorily, due to the old king's endurance? Now he was cheered by the wife he loved, and consoled by the Church which he had served so faithfully. Surrounded by devoted attendants, he confidently waited the call to an even more exalted mansion than Versailles. So goes the story, and perhaps there is some truth in it. Yet there are also grounds for thinking that the Sun King's last days were often sad and trying.

Louis' magnificent constitution had now been undermined by old age and the doctors. Unfortunately Louis never possessed the common sense of Elizabeth I of England who remained healthy because she refused to listen to her doctors. Louis XIV by contrast was meekly obedient to his medical advisers, and paid dearly for it. His old age was plagued by rheumatism, indigestion and gout. Furthermore, a clumsy dentist had removed half of Louis' jaw, so that he could not chew his vast meals.

The ineptitude of doctors and dentists in days gone by encourages us to count our blessings. Nancy Mitford has written sceptically of the medical profession that 'in those days, terrifying in black robes and bonnets, they bled the patient; now, terrifying in white robes and masks, they pump blood into him'. But when she argues that 'the result is the same', evidence such as the present expectation of life is against her. Truly horrifying was the dominance exercised by Louis XIV's doctor, the arrogant and bungling charlatan Guy-Crescent Fagon whom Madame de Maintenon imposed on him. Fagon compounded the pain which his royal patient suffered from gout and other ailments by prescribing unpleasant and harmful medicines and imposing endless purgings and bleedings. Thanks to this 'treatment' by the end of his life Louis was an emaciated shell of his former self.

However, the ravages wrought by Fagon on Louis' own health distressed him less than the damage done to the rest of the royal family. As we have seen, three dauphins were killed off by Fagon in 11 months - and the fact that in order to conceal his own incompetence Fagon encouraged the rumour that they had been poisoned by Orleans, the king's nephew, does not increase one's respect for him. Louis was further prostrated with grief when his grandson's wife, the duchesse de Burgundy, also fell a victim to a combination of measles and Fagon's cures. Marie-Adelaide - she who curtseyed so badly - had been the particular favourite of the king and his ageing wife. She was affectionate, vivacious and just a little cheeky; she brought life and laughter into the old people's staid existence, and they adored her. And now she too was gone. Louis was naturally warm-hearted and loved young people; *toujours les enfants* ('children always to be in evidence') he had directed Le Nôtre when Versailles was being planned. So of course he was heartbroken by these bereavements. Furthermore, not only did the slaughter of the younger generation upset Louis as an affectionate head of the family, but he believed that these tragedies indicated divine wrath because of the sexual dalliances of his youth.

The state of the nation gave cause for concern as well. Isolated though he was at Versailles, Louis could not be totally unaware of the deplorable plight of his people, nor of the fact that he was blamed for it. True, the wars had finished. But the damaging effects on France could not quickly or easily be erased. The Crown was over 2,000 million livres in debt. Taxation remained high, agriculture and trade were in the doldrums, thousands had been bereaved during the wars, and the walking wounded were everywhere. It was only to be expected that abroad pamphleteers and cartoonists mocked the Sun King, rejoicing at his discomfiture and alleging that he was now an impotent old fool:

> The plagues of war and wife consent
> To send the king a packing;
> You cannot give your spouse content,
> For she'll be always lacking.

Even the French now repeated rhymes blaming Louis for the disasters affecting the nation and for his subordination to Madame de Maintenon.

> One could without being satirical
> Even find this regime comical.
> See how this holy whore
> Directs this whole empire.
> If we were not dying of hunger,
> We would die of laughter.

A parody of the Lord's Prayer ran as follows: 'Our father who art at Versailles, thy name is no longer hallowed, thy realm is no longer great, thy will is no longer done on earth or at sea. Give us today our daily bread which we totally lack. Forgive our enemies who have defeated us, and our generals who have allowed them to do this. Deliver us from Chamillart and de Maintenon'.

Nevertheless, despite such widespread criticism and the bankruptcy of the royal treasury, Versailles was still maintained in splendour and foreign embassies were still received with no expense spared. Music and drama were still presented for his majesty's delight. But no-one could escape the impression that the sparkle and the vitality of former years had departed. Life at Versailles now was joyless and tedious. Everyone waited for the supreme actor to leave his stage.

In the summer of 1715 Louis XIV was clearly far from well. He had lost his appetite and found it difficult to sleep, which was not surprising as Fagon insisted on the king wrapping himself in feather bedding to make him sweat. In August the king's leg began to hurt him and black spots appeared. Fagon diagnosed sciatica, though everyone else knew it was gangrene. Eventually Fagon prescribed amputation. Louis for once defied his doctor: 'I'm too old for surgery and not afraid to die'.

The Sun King's death was gruesome and prolonged. Needless to say it occurred in public, and equally predictably Louis suffered with courage and dignity. Truly he had much to suffer. Madame de Maintenon badgered the dying man not only to confess *all* his sins but to add a codicil to his will, putting the duc de Maine in charge of the future Louis XV's education. The noise of the ladies of the court wailing in the next room - they were expected to do this - prevented Louis sleeping. 'Do they think I'm immortal?' he pleaded. At last the end came on 1 September 1715. Louis asked his courtiers to forgive him for setting them such a bad example. He blessed the little boy who was to succeed him, advising him not to copy his excessive love of building and of warfare. 'I had no idea dying was so easy' he whispered to Madame de Maintenon who constantly watched by his bed. After drinking one last quack remedy Louis XIV slipped away murmuring 'God help me'.

Although the funeral was performed with magnificent formality, a mob insulted the corpse. However, pulpits thundered and re-echoed all over France with fulsome praise of the dead king. Perhaps a more meaningful and sincere comment came from the court. Within hours of the Sun King's death, the great palace of Versailles was empty. Everyone had gone home.

2 Assessment

a) Louis the Man

'It is impossible not to respect him, but equally impossible to like him'. Readers will recall this tentative judgement of Louis XIV, which I suggested as a basis for discussion in the Introduction. Perhaps there are grounds for modifying this judgement.

While anyone must respect Louis' professionalism, devotion to duty, self-control, courage and dignity, whether one actually likes him is a matter of personal opinion. Without presuming to judge Louis XIV, attractive qualities can be recognised in the Sun King's make-up. While Louis could behave arrogantly and insentitively, he had many good points. He could be thoughtful and kind. He had a warm heart. He was a generous and considerate employer. He was kind to people such as the exiled James II who were down on their luck. He was not naturally vindictive or cruel.

Furthermore, Louis XIV was such a civilised man. It was not merely that he defended Molière and had nice manners. His courtesy was founded on basic tolerance and genuine good humour which he consistently revealed in his private relationships. So far as his public acts were concerned, it is true that on occasions he displayed ruthlessness, arrogance and religious bigotry. However, one could not conceive of him behaving like Carlos II who presided in person over the public burning of 18 heretics in Madrid on 30 June 1680. When Philip V proposed to massacre some captured rebels in Barcelona, Louis wrote to his grandson to remonstrate against such barbarity.

The corrupting influences of power, success and adulation were countered in Louis' old age by disaster, failure and bereavement. To his credit he did not resort to self-pity, he did not blame others, and he did not curse God and die. The Sun King's courage, serenity and humility when the weather turned foul surely entitle him both to our respect and our sympathy. Overall, one can even like him.

b) Louis XIV's Record as King of France

1 My child, you are about to become a great king. Do not imitate my
  love of building nor my liking for war, but try, on the contrary, to
  live at peace with your neighbours. Render to God all that you owe
  Him; recognise your duty towards Him; see that He is honoured by
5 your subjects. Always follow good counsellors; try to comfort your
  people, which it grieves me that I have been unable to do.

Until recently historians have taken their cue from Saint-Simon's description of the dying Louis XIV's advice to his youthful successor. In particular, they have agreed with the Sun King's self-condemnation for his extravagant building and excessive love of war. However, revisionists have doubted whether Louis really said anything of the sort - Saint-Simon's notorious dislike of his royal master makes him an unreliable witness - and have questioned the justice of such criticisms whether Louis expressed them or not.

What cannot be denied is the dominance which Louis XIV's foreign policy exercised over domestic policy - and which some critics would regard as deplorable and excessive. In pursuit of *la gloire* the Sun King sought to defend the reputation of his House on the battlefield and to make France more secure by defeating her enemies and acquiring strategically important territory. Domestic policy was subordinate to these paramount goals. Thus administrative and economic initiatives had to be postponed and financial prudence had to be jettisoned so that money could be raised to pay for the king's wars. It is therefore a crucial question whether Louis XIV's involvement in so much warfare was necessary. Were the goals achieved worth all that blood, time and effort, to say nothing of the postponement of necessary initiatives at home?

Could those same objectives have been gained by other, more intelligent tactics which might have permitted desirable domestic reforms, making France a happier and better governed state?

The territorial objectives of Louis XIV's foreign policy were not unreasonable, nor were his net gains on France's behalf contemptible. At the height of his success in the late 1680s he had in his grasp even more valuable acquisitions than those he was allowed to keep by the Utrecht settlement. Historians who defend Louis XIV's foreign policy point out that precisely because these gains were so important his enemies bitterly contested them. Hence it is arguable that Louis' early wars were fought for sensible, necessary objectives, while the later wars were imposed on him by France's enemies, determined not to allow her to become secure. Thus Louis XIV can be acquitted of the charge of being an irresponsible warmonger; if he did plead guilty on his deathbed to this charge, he was not being fair to himself.

However, some would argue that such a defence is too kind to Louis XIV. First, the evidence convicts him of causing the Dutch War of 1672 for frivolous, irresponsible motives of pride and revenge. Secondly, Louis' foreign policy in the 1680s was provocative and insensitive; if, as his defenders claim, his enemies imputed to him aggressive ambitions which he did not hold, they had good reason for misunderstanding him. Thirdly, Louis showed poor tactical sense after Carlos II's will was published in 1700 leaving his empire to Louis' grandson. Louis almost seemed to wish on himself the great coalition which challenged Carlos' will and brought France to her knees. A further point: if Louis was not a bloodthirsty or a callous man, he none the less was too ready to resort to war. He was too quick to take the short cut and appeal to violence - a criticism which in fact applies both to his foreign and domestic policies.

Another argument put forward by Louis XIV's advocates brings us to the heart of the matter: his foreign policy was a continuation of the robust assertions of French nationalism by the cardinals. If Richelieu and Mazarin are admired for their pursuit of nationally desirable objectives, why should Louis XIV be blamed for resorting to war for the same reasons? But the point here is that the contrast between Louis XIV and the cardinals is as striking as the similarity. Granted that there is the same aggressive pursuit of French national interests. Granted that the cardinals were oblivious to human suffering and as ruthless as the Sun King. But one misses in Louis XIV the logical, well thought-out strategy of Richelieu and Mazarin. The fact is that he was strategically and tactically second rate. There is no coherently worked-out list of priorities, no ability to see beyond the next over-clever piece of opportunism. One cannot see Richelieu alienating the papacy when the Archbishopric of Cologne was in the balance. Nor would Mazarin have heedlessly thrown away the support of the German princes at the same time as quarrelling with the Emperor.

Equally contrasting is the flexible realism of the cardinals and Louis

XIV's doctrinal rigidity. Ironically Louis was far more prejudiced against Protestants than the two princes of the Church who gladly recruited Swedish, Dutch and German heretics to help France. While Richelieu and Mazarin tolerated the Huguenots, Louis persecuted them - the greatest blot on his record. Equally doctrinaire was his refusal to take cognisance of public opinion abroad, for only the regard of his fellow monarchs was of significance. Excessive devotion to the divine right of kings prompted Louis to one of his major blunders, the recognition of James the Old Pretender when James II died in 1701.

'Try to comfort your people which it grieves me I have been unable to do.' Did Louis XIV indeed neglect the welfare of his eighteen and a half million subjects? It might seem perverse to forgive the cardinals for pursuing national objectives at the expense of domestic reform, but to blame Louis XIV for the same 'crime'. But Louis had so much more opportunity to do good, to achieve something worthwhile for France. His position as King of France was immeasurably stronger than the cardinals'. Yet he failed to utilise this strength for the good of his people. It is not simply that he allowed himself to be involved in expensive wars which necessitated desirable reforms being put on the back-burner, for he could have achieved considerable success both at home and abroad. In other words, it was not necessarily a case of 'either/or'. For there is a fundamental blindness and obtuseness in Louis XIV which prevented him from identifying the right priorities.

By his own lights Louis XIV was extremely successful as ruler of France; basically he got what he wanted - apart from those military defeats at the end of the reign. Inside France Louis established himself as the master, so that he was able to rule in the style which he found conducive. Whether we call it absolutism or not, Louis XIV and his ministers were able to decide policy and summon the means to put it into effect, including above all the money to fund it. While there were limitations on the king's power, by and large Louis was able to do whatever he wanted in the areas that mattered to him.

For instance he enjoyed establishing the paraphernalia of monarchy, living the expensive and luxurious life which he believed was appropriate, enabling his ever-expanding family to share this lifestyle with him. From 1688 Louis added the court of the exiled James II of England to his own domestic pay-roll. And why not? Divine-right was thus publicly defended, while Louis' courtiers admired the spectacle.

As for the rest of France, what did Louis XIV really care about? Two things. First, there was to be no threat of armed rebellion, especially under aristocratic leadership. Here the Sun King's success was complete; set against the disorders of previous reigns, he was brilliant. Secondly, and closely connected with his outlawing of rebellion, was intellectual and religious conformity. Here Louis XIV was less successful. Nevertheless, his obstinate authoritarianism was formidable enough to drive criticism and dissent underground; he failed to suppress the Huguenots, but made life exceedingly unpleasant for them. While the Sun King lived, France remained an orthodox and cowed nation. A few sharp-shooters sniped from abroad at Louis's magnificent edifice of total conformity. Fenelon wrote the king rude letters - but never sent them. In truth, Louis achieved his ambitions.

However, surely Louis XIV got it wrong. The ball was in his court, and he could have achieved just about any aims which he set himself. In these circumstances, can one accept that his priorities were right? Is there evidence of the necessary self-discipline, husbanding of resources and intelligent long-term strategy which France needed?

Look at France in 1715 when Louis XIV died. The government was bankrupt and the national economy was ravaged by war and the resulting high taxation. There had been no attempt to emulate the British and the Dutch who had discovered how to finance war by long-term, low interest borrowing. French agriculture was still primitive and inefficient. Virtually none of the handicaps and anomalies which cluttered up the French state in 1661 had been removed. Despite Colbert's legal reforms, there was still no consistency or logic in the administration of justice; seigneurial courts, church courts, royal courts, and town and village courts competed with each other. Similar chaos affected external and internal trade; a multiplicity of tolls, tariffs and dues impeded enterprise and the pursuit of profit, so that England and Scotland still constituted the largest common market in Europe. Taxation was still the unjust, corrupt and wasteful mess that it had been half a century earlier; despite the *capitation* and the *dixième*, which barely touched the problem, the rich were exempt and the poor were crucified. France was still a grotesque class society, based on privilege and snobbery. The equation of Colbert with 'good sense' has this validity: Colbert with all his blind-spots showed occasional understanding of the needs of the French people - which is more than can be said for Louis XIV.

Of the obituaries pronounced on the Sun King, the most perceptive came from the pen of the parish priest at Saint-Sulpice, near Blois:

1 Louis XIV, King of France and Navarre, died on September 1 of this year, scarcely regretted by his whole kingdom, on account of the exorbitant sums and heavy taxes he levied on his subjects. It is not permitted to repeat all the verses, all the songs, or all the
5 unfavourable comments which have been written or said against his memory. During his life he was so absolute, that he passed all the laws to do his will. The princes and the nobles were repressed, the *parlements* had no power; it was obligatory to receive and register all edicts, since the king was so powerful and so absolute.
10 The clergy were shamefully servile in doing the King's will. Only the moneylenders and tax-collectors were at peace, living joyfully with all the money of the kingdom in their possession.

c) 'A Great King'?

It might be thought that 'greatness' is an unsatisfactory concept for a historian, too vague, too much a question of personal values and preferences. One is reminded of Andrew Bonar Law, the British Prime Minister: 'If I am a great man, then I suspect that all great men are frauds'. Nevertheless, Louis XIV allowed his media specialists to call him 'Great' and therefore in a sense he puts us on the spot, challenging us to agree or disagree. It is thought-provoking that in the event the title 'Great' did *not* stick; by contrast Louis' contemporary Tsar Peter's 'Greatness' *was* duly acknowledged, both by contemporaries and posterity. Yet at the same time even hostile historians describe Louis XIV as 'a great king'

So what does it mean to call a king 'great'? If one avoids personal opinion, 'greatness' must surely involve introducing radical changes, turning the world upside down, leaving it a very different place - and perhaps a better place? Here the welfare of a king's subjects is relevant, if it can be objectively established. 'Greatness' also involves a monarch's personal qualities, his courage in adversity, his mercy to defeated opponents, his modesty in the face of success.

If we accept these criteria, the most relevant piece of evidence must be the Sun King's legacy to France. As we have seen, France's internal situation at Louis XIV's death was depressing, for he had ignored the grave social, economic, legal and administrative problems facing the nation. Instead, he had established a tradition of warfare in the pursuit of national objectives whatever the cost. One historian has justifiably written that Louis bequeathed to his people 'a legacy of bankruptcy and glamour'. He also bequeathed the messy and bitter Jansenist controversy to the French Church. And he imposed on his successors an unsatisfactory political system; as a result of the repression of rival sources of authority there was no satisfactory way in which constructive criticism of the government could be expressed.

The contrast with Peter the Great is instructive. When it came to real national priorities Louis XIV totally lacked the forward-looking vision of that terrifying autocrat. It has been said that Louis caused the French Revolution which swept away his great-great-grandson. While it is absurd to blame someone for events over 70 years after his death and while Louis' successors had plenty of opportunities to put matters right, Louis certainly failed to tackle the flaws in the *ancien régime* which contributed to the ultimate debacle.

Even where Louis XIV was indisputably great, in the field of style, self-presentation and propaganda, it can be argued that his success harmed him more than it helped him. For not only did he dazzle contemporaries and posterity, but he also dazzled himself. All the 'hype' of the Versailles media industry blinded Louis XIV to reality, making it harder for him to identify priorities and shielding him from unpleasant realities. The 'fabrication' of Louis XIV was both a sign of insecurity and a cause of arrogance and self-deception.

And what of Louis XIV's exercise of kingly power? Do not his devotion to duty, his professionalism, his efficiency in establishing his will amount to greatness? Perhaps. But again it is arguable that Louis' very strengths carried with them corresponding weaknesses. Thus he was too much involved in detail to see the wood for the trees. In fact Louis XIV's decision to be his own chief minister was probably a mistake. Alternatively, if he was determined to be chief minister he had to make the regular recruitment of new men with new ideas an absolute priority. Whatever his advice may have been to his great-grandson, he himself consulted counsellors who became more and more mediocre. As a result his rule became ossified and uninspired.

Lack of inspiration! This is perhaps the crucial flaw which militates against Louis' claims to greatness. Far from taking the long view and perceiving the requirements of France in the future, Louis XIV was the worst kind of conservative. Partly because he lived so long, he became increasingly old-fashioned and out of touch. He was the prisoner of history rather than its creator, for he was in a real sense the product of previous centuries. His religious hang-ups, his social conservatism, his inability to grasp economic priorities all brand him as a man out of his depth in a changing world. While it would be foolish to blame Louis XIV for his background or his intellectual limitations, his inability to think creatively and with forward-looking vision made him a second-rate ruler.

But what is one to expect from such an unsatisfactory system as hereditary monarchy? Louis XIV's contemporary, the Earl of Halifax, remarked that no-one would appoint his coachman on such a principle. If a man is unlikely to guide a coach well because he is his father's eldest son, what chance had Louis XIV of guiding a great nation? To adapt Henri IV's verdict on Catherine de Medici, it is astonishing that he did not do worse. In Louis' case the problem was exacerbated because there is no retiring age for monarchs; as we have seen, the Sun King himself discovered that a long life is not necessarily a happy one, while his people longed for the end of the reign.

So if a hereditary monarch such as Louis XIV was unlikely to be great, what was the answer? The French revolutionaries guillotined Louis XVI, the English executed Charles I. However, the Sun King's English contemporaries eventually combined a monarchy of sorts with the representative institutions which Louis XIV so successfully snuffed out. Wistful envy of the English concludes one of the subversive ditties circulating in Paris towards the end of the reign:

Le grandpère est un fanfaron,
Le fils un imbecile,
Le petit fils un grand poltron,
Ohe! la belle famille.

> Que je vous plains, pauvres Francais,
> Soumis a cest empire.
> Faites comme ont fait les Anglais,
> C'est assez vous en dire.

(The grandfather is a braggart, the son an imbecile, the grandson an utter wimp, oh dear! what a lovely family. How I pity you, poor French people, having to submit to this regime. Do as the English have done, that's good enough advice for you.)

Nevertheless, it would be wrong to close on such a negative, churlish note. Louis XIV fascinated and dominated his world. He must have had elements of greatness. He was a magnificent king and a decent human being. Let one of his bereaved courtiers, with typical hyperbole, have the last word: 'After the death of the king, anything is possible'.

Making notes on the *Conclusion*

It is not necessary to make many notes on the first section of this chapter which rounds off the reign in a narrative way; it is to be read and absorbed. However, the last two sections could with profit be noted. Summarise the arguments for and against Louis XIV as a professional monarch. How good at his job was he? Were his approaches to the challenge of ruling France the right ones? Evaluate the Sun King as a man-manager and as a decision-maker. Summarise the validity of his perceptions as to what France really needed. Note Louis XIV's legacy to France. With these criteria in mind make your own estimation of Louis XIV's claims to greatness. Compiling these notes will indeed concentrate your mind. A further piece of advice: my experience of teaching this topic leads me to the conclusion that one of the best ways of assessing Louis XIV's achievement is to write an essay on his record as a whole (see next section). If you have not done this, ask your teacher to set you a suitable question.

Answering essay questions on the *Conclusion*

To a great extent examiners concentrate on specific aspects of Louis XIV's reign, such as his foreign policy, his approach to government, and his impact on the economic or religious life of France.

However, just occasionally you might be asked to agree or disagree with the suggestion that Louis was a great king. This issue is discussed in the Conclusion. It is a fascinating question. But be warned, it is also a dangerous area where it is only too easy to play God, preach, display bias, waffle or go off the point. You need a strictly matter-of-fact introduction in order to avoid catastrophe: perhaps you might stress that not even Frenchmen ultimately have accepted that Louis XIV was 'great', that 'greatness' is a matter of opinion, and (most importantly of all) that for the purposes of this essay you have to lay down your own criteria for greatness in order to avoid sketchy generalisations.

You might also be asked to discuss Louis XIV's legacy to France. This is also discussed in the Conclusion. It too is a fascinating question. It is more straightforward than the 'greatness' issue, but do remember that you require a clear grasp of the eighteenth-century consequences of Louis' reign if you are to answer such a question successfully.

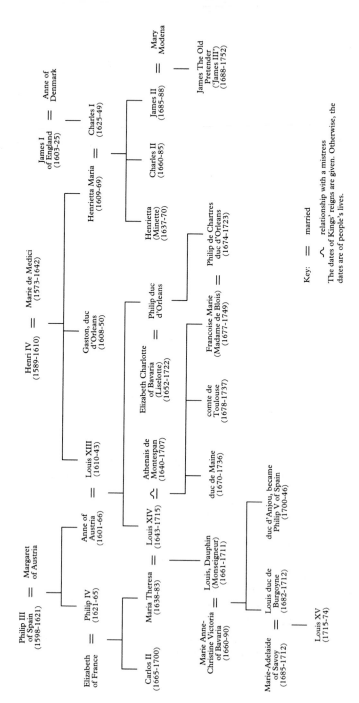

The Family of Louis XIV

Chronological Tables

1638	5 Sept.	Birth of Louis XIV.
1643	14 May	Death of Louis XIII. Regency of Anne of Austria.
1648-53		The *Frondes* revolts.
1659	Nov.	Treaty of the Pyrenees ended war between France and Spain.
1660	June	Marriage of Louis XIV and Maria Theresa.
1661	9 Mar.	Death of Mazarin. The beginning of the personal rule.
	Sep.	Arrest and disgrace of Fouquet.
1662	Apr.	Dunkirk purchased from England.
1663-70		French trading companies founded.
1664	Apr.	Archbishop of Paris visited Port Royale.
1664	May	The Pleasures of the Enchanted Isle at Versailles.
1667	May	War of Devolution - French invasion of the Spanish Netherlands.
1668	May	Peace of Aix-la-Chapelle between France and Spain.
1670	June	The Treaty of Dover between France and England.
1672	June	The Dutch War. French invasion of Holland.
1675	May	Peasant revolt in Brittany.
1678-9		The Treaties of Nymegen concluded the Dutch War.
1680-3		The Reunions.
1681	Sept.	Seizure of Strasburg.
1682		Death of Colbert.
1682	Mar.	Gallican Articles attacked the Pope's authority in France.
1682	May	The Court moved to Versailles.
1683	July	Death of Maria Theresa.
1684	Aug.	Truce of Ratisbon confirmed French acquisitions.
1685	Oct.	Edict of Fontainebleau: Edict of Nantes revoked.
1688	Sept.	The Cologne election: French candidate defeated.
1688-9		Devastation of the Palatinate.
1688-97		The Nine Years War.
1697	Oct.	Treaty of Ryswick ended the Nine Years War.
1699	July	Foundation of Louisiana.
1700	1 Nov.	The death of Carlos II of Spain. Publication of his will.
1702-13		War of the Spanish Succession.
1702-4		Camisard revolt, caused by persecution of Huguenots.
1704	Aug.	Battle of Blenheim.
1705	July	The papal Bull *Vineam Domini* condemned Jansenism.
1708-9		Terrible winter devastated France.

1710		*Dixième* (income tax) imposed.
1711	July	Victory of Denain: Villars defeated Eugene.
1711-12		The Dauphin, and the duc and duchesse de Burgundy died.
1713	Mar.	Treaty of Utrecht ended the War of the Spanish Succession.
1713	Sept.	The papal Bull *Unigenitus* was issued. It was an even more severe attack on Jansenism.
1715	1 Sept.	Death of Louis XIV.

The Reign of Louis XIV in context

1559-89	The last Valois kings. Marie de Medici regent.
1563-98	French Wars of Religion.
1589-1610	Reign of Henri IV (Henri of Navarre - the first Bourbon)
1598	The Edict of Nantes.
1610-43	Reign of Louis XIII.
1624-42	Cardinal Richelieu chief minister.
1618-48	Thirty Years War in Germany.
1630-1719	The Baltic dominated by Sweden.
1642-9	English civil wars.
1643-61	Cardinal Mazarin chief minister.
1648	Treaty of Westphalia (Treaty of Munster).
1648-1750	Gradual decline of Spain.
1649	Execution of Charles I of England.
1660	Restoration of Charles II.
1665	Death of Philip IV of Spain. Accession of Carlos II.
1687	Battle of Mohacs: Leopold defeated the Turks.
1688-9	The English Revolution: William III's invasion.
1689-1776	The foundation of the British Empire.
1714	The Elector of Hanover became George I, King of Great Britain.
1715-74	Reign of Louis XV.
1774-93	Reign of Louis XVI.
1776	The American revolt against Great Britain began.
1789	Outbreak of the French Revolution.

Further Reading

a) Original sources

Saint-Simon's *Memoirs* are incomparable: great fun, although not always reliable. Read them in the original French if you can, but Lucy Norton's edited translation is a useful second best (Hamish Hamilton 1958). **Roger Mettam's** *Government and Society in Louis XIV's France* (Macmillan 1977) is an invaluable collection of documents illustrating how France was governed.

b) Biographies

A sensible way to supplement this book is to read a biography of Louis XIV. There are several. Nowadays historians tend to disparage **David Ogg's** biography which is inevitably out-of-date (published by Home University Library in 1933). But it still reads well and is seldom misleading. **Vincent Cronin's** *Louis XIV* (Pan paperback 1969) is pleasantly readable. Perhaps the best all-round attempt (scholarly, based on original research but quite accessible to the general reader) is still **J. B. Wolf's** *Louis XIV* (London 1969). And then there is **F. Bluche!** (Blackwell 1990). Originally written by a Frenchman for Frenchmen this is well translated and enjoyable enough. But it is very long and very biased in the Sun King's favour - no bad thing really for Anglo-Saxon readers. **Nancy Mitford's** *The Sun King* is enjoyable as a literary romp.

c) Textbooks

The present work should remove the necessity to consult general European textbooks on this topic. However, it might be worth consulting **G.R.R. Treasure's** *Seventeenth Century France* (Longman 1961) and **W.E. Brown's** *The First Bourbon Century* (London 1968). In addition, the Historical Association pamphlet *Louis XIV* by **Roland Mousnier** and the Lancaster University pamphlet by **J.H. Shannon** are both excellent.

d) Specialist studies worth reading include:

Robin Briggs, *Early Modern France* (Oxford 1977)
Robin Briggs, *Communities of Belief* (Oxford 1989)
Peter Burke, *The Fabrication of Louis XIV* (Yale 1992)

Pierre Goubert, *Louis XIV and Twenty Million Frenchmen* (London 1973)

Ragnhild Hatton, *Louis XIV and his World* (Thames and Hudson 1972)

Ragnhild Hatton, *Louis XIV and Europe* (Macmillan 1976)

Roger Mettam, *Power and Faction in Louis XIV's France* (Blackwell 1988)

David Parker, *The Making of French Absolutism* (London 1983)

W.S. Scovill, *The Persecution of the Huguenots and French Economic Development* (California 1960)

J.C. Rule, *Louis XIV and the Craft of Kingship* (Ohio 1969)

Paul Sonnino, (Ed), *The Reign of Louis XIV* (Essays) (London 1990)

Acknowledgements

The publishers would like to thank the following for permission to reproduce illustrations in this volume:

Cover and page 85, Services de la Réunion Photographique des Musées Nationaux, Paris; page 86 (top), Mansell Collection; page 86 (bottom), British Library, London.

Many people have helped me to write this short book. In particular, Robin Briggs of All Souls College, Oxford and Roger Mettam of the University of London gave me generously of their time; if I have not profited from their guidance, the fault is mine. I have enjoyed working with David Lea and Clare Weaver of Hodder and Stoughton. Keith Randell has been an inspiring and constructive editor who has saved me from countless errors. I am grateful for the support of my family, especially my wife who has checked the proofs. I dedicate the book to her - the least I can do!

Index

Readers seeking a specific piece of information might find it helpful to consult the *Contents* and the *Chronological Tables* as well as this brief *Index*.